TALES FROM THE RANKS AND BEYOND

By Roger I. Lewis

Copyright © 2015 R.I. Lewis

The right of Roger I. Lewis to be identified as the Author of the Work has been asserted by him in accordance with the Copyright, Designs and Patents Act 1988.

First published by Roger I. Lewis Publishing

Apart from any use permitted under UK copyright law, this publication may only be reproduced, stored, or transmitted, in any form, or by any means, with prior permission in writing of the publishers or Author himself or, in the case of reprographic production, in accordance with the terms of the licences issued by the Copyright Licencing Agency.

A format (ISBN 978-0-9935205-1-8)

Printed by Fearless Creative

Dedications

This book is dedicated to my ten Grandchildren
Ethan, Oscar, Marley, Phoebe, Felix, Farrah,
Cyd, Ava, Poppy and Pebbles.

Acknowledgements

Allison Laird for editorial work;

Polly Sullivan for proof reading and layout;

Lance Everett for cover design;

Paul Mitchell for reminding me of forgotten stories that he has heard one hundred times before.

PREFACE

When a man grows old he recounts his lifetime stories, and his close companions have heard them all, quite a few times. I want my tales to reach my ten grandchildren when they are old enough to appreciate them, and that when they read this it will bring a smile to their faces. Every city, town and village has its own characters but none more so than the big cities and none more so than London. It was my privilege to be born and bred in inner London and to mix with some great personalities: some loveable rogues, some criminals and some great family people. In short, people from all walks of life. I hope these tales teach them about their family history and the characters encountered growing up and growing old in an exciting time.

In 1949, when I was nearly seven years old, I first realised love for a man, a love that lasted another fifty seven years until he died at eighty eight years of age. I was at St Bede's

Deaf Club at Clapham North, and there was a man there in his forties, his hair slicked back with a centre parting - fashionable at the time - and he sat in a chair staring ahead. His name was Frank and he was blind, deaf and unable to speak. Even at seven I was full of sympathy for this man in darkness who was unable to hear. Then I saw my Dad, Lenny Lewis, walk over to him, pat him on the back, take his hand, introduce himself and proceed to hold communication, ending with a joke which left Frank's shoulders heaving with laughter. All this was achieved by sign language on Frank's hand and was his only communication and pleasure in life.

From that day on my Dad was my hero, and it taught me to be considerate to those less fortunate than myself.

You see, I had what you might call an unusual upbringing. Both my parents were profoundly deaf. At an early age I was communicating in sign language, although I could hear, and through my parents I mixed with deaf people whose kindness and openness I remember to this day. It was an unusual upbringing in another way as well: I was the product of a mixed marriage between a Jewish top presser and a Church of England seamstress. It was down to this, I believe, that taught me to see the funny side of things, something I picked up from my Parents and Grandparents and to whom I am eternally grateful.

Back in the forties, deaf people referred to themselves as 'deaf and dumb'. Today the term is 'profoundly deaf'. Whatever the term, deaf people had to overcome their handicap and make a decent lifestyle for themselves and their families. To be brought up in a rough area of London gave me the best education at the 'University of Life', giving me the common sense to survive for seventy-three years, and make a good living along the way.

CONTENTS

1	Family and Growing Up	13
2	Swinging Sixties	109
3	Stories, Characters and Likeable Rogues	135
4	On My Travels	171
5	Covent Garden Market	184
6	The Knowledge	204
7	Cab Driving – A Noble Profession	222
8	The Royals	246
9	Cab Stories	248
10	LTDA – Licensed Taxi Drivers' Association	311
11	South-East Golf Society	342
12	The Mafia	347
13	The Movies and Me	351
14	The Three Ladies	363
	Appendix	372
	Rest in Peace	382

CHAPTER ONE
Family and Growing Up

It is often remarked that historically the East End is London's counterpart to Ellis Island. For it is to the East End that immigrants and refugees first arrive on these shores. So it was for both sets of my grandparents.

Nathaniel Matthew Kapelnekoff was born in the Ukraine, in the city of Kiev, on 21 February 1890. He was one of the two million Jews who, fearing for their lives, fled the Russian Empire between 1880 and 1914, emigrating to either the UK or the United States. In the Ukraine, the pogroms and anti-Jewish riots of 1903 – 1905 were especially savage and hundreds of villages throughout the Ukraine were torched and Jews murdered in their thousands. Quite understandably, either my Grandad had had enough or maybe he could see the writing on the wall. He aimed to join his older siblings who were already in America, but, at one point when the ship docked, he disembarked in London, having been told he was in New York City. The year was 1908. He slept under the barrows of Petticoat Lane and somehow made a good living before he married Esther, sometime in 1914 in Bishopsgate in the City of London.

My Grandmother Esther's maiden name was Richovitch. She was born in Lithuania in 1890 and from there she emigrated to London with her family, again, because of the pogroms. Grandma Lewis, as I called her, was a kindly soul who doted on her family, serving delicious kosher food. Her specialties were cakes and biscuits. Even into her late seventies, before she died ill with diabetes in St Francis Hospital, Dulwich, she spoke with a heavy accent. I was with my Dad at her bedside when she died.

My Grandad Nat became a successful stall holder in Petticoat Lane and the 'Blue' in Bermondsey just south of Tower Bridge. He was a good salesman with great patter.

Some people say that the first superstar was Harry Lauder, the Scottish singer who took America by storm. Grandad frequented the music halls, and would often sing Harry Lauder's Scottish songs to me when I was a nipper. Little did I know that, in later life, I would be living in Scotland.

A favourite joke of his was the teacher asked the class to draw a wicker basket. After a while, she stopped at a little boy's desk to see a sketch of Hitler! "What's that, George? I told you to draw a wicker basket."

"Sorry, Miss," came the reply, "I thought you said a wicked bastard!"

Of my Mother's parents, Frank and Edith Rogers, Frank was a 'dyed in the wool' Cockney and Edith was a descendant of the Huguenots, sometimes called Britain's first refugees - French Protestants forced to flee in their tens of thousands to Britain, firstly in the late seventeenth century and then again in 1789 to escape the guillotine. As everyone knows, Huguenots were highly skilled weavers and made a good life for themselves in their adopted countries.

It all began for me in 1939, when the little bastard with the moustache and fringe ended peace in our time and, likewise, a certain marriage did the same in the East End of London. Mixed marriages between Jews and non-Jews were frowned upon and this one became the subject of a bitter dispute between my two sets of Grandparents. Despite the almighty row between the two families, common sense finally prevailed, with my Grandad Frank finally winning the day by stating that the young couple, my parents Len and Amy, had been 'courting' for three years, obviously loved each other, and were not going to accept the taboo of mixed marriage.

In due course, I made my debut on 16 December 1942. As my Grandad Nat Kapellnekoff had taken his father's name 'Lewis' as his surname when he married my Grandmother, and as Frank and Edith's last name was Rogers, I was named Roger Lewis, with the distinctively Russian middle name of Ivan. I was their only child because, as they would explain later in life, their friends were both profoundly deaf and had a son my age who could hear, then had twins who were both deaf. So Mum and Dad weren't taking any chances with another child. My Son took the time to look at the genetics and found that if both parents had a certain gene, it could mean deafness for the child.

As soon as I made my appearance, unbeknownst to me as a mere baby, there was another almighty battle brewing for the way I was to be brought up. Nat and Esther wanted their only son's wife to be Jewish and their only grandson to be brought up in that religion. Nat brought in the Mohel and I was circumcised. I can't remember if it was painful, but I always thought the wrong part was thrown away!

Unfortunately, my Mum was never really accepted by her in-laws, and the term used was 'shiksa' (non-Jewish lady). So I walked a fine line until I was old enough to make my mind up as to which direction I wanted to travel in.

Out of love for both my Parents I declined both religions, and never adopted either. My Father had been unable to have a Barmitzvah because of the spoken part of the ritual and accepted my reason for abstaining: in the Jewish way a Jew has to be born of a Jew, and my Mother wasn't. So the years between birth and the age of thirteen (Barmitzvah time) were always a constant battle between the two families. After the thirteen years had passed I was left alone and things became easier.

I loved both sets of my Grandparents and was spoiled by them on visits. In Bermondsey, on the south side of the river, Esther and Nat would give me wonderful kosher food, beautiful cakes and my favourite drink as a kid – Tizer. Meanwhile, from their East End roots, Eadie and Frank would teach me Cockney-speak and principles, introduce me to jellied eels, pie and mash, boiled beef and carrots, pease pudding and sometimes a small glass of beer to wash it down.

As I got older I only went to Synagogue for weddings, Barmitzvahs and funerals. I managed to remain neutral and was loved by both sets of Grandparents, despite my non-commitment. The two families imparted their ways and lifestyles on me which taught me good values for my formative years and gave me a resilience for the jobs I held in later life at the top of demanding associations.

My Father

My Father, Lennie Lewis, was born in 1916 during the First World War. He never heard or spoke a word all his life, as he had been born with damaged ear drums, but he had the knack of being in your company for a few minutes and made you smile and warm to him. His sister Phyllis was born two years later and was talking, but my Dad had not uttered a word. That was the first indication to my Grandparents Lewis that something was wrong.

My Dad was proud of the fact that he was never late for work in all his working days. He never had a good night's sleep and was constantly keeping his eye on the bedside clock. Then one day his pal brought him a flashing clock which was heaven sent. On top of his clock watching, he would wake up at intervals to see if my suit jacket was hanging on his bedroom door. This was because on one occasion I forgot my street door key and couldn't get into the flat. So, thinking of me standing outside in all weathers, he insisted I put my coat on his bedroom door to let him know I was in. It also let him know the lateness of my getting home if I got lucky.

A popular innovation for deaf people in the 1960s was a flashing light in the parlour when the door bell was pressed. But my Dad had the ultimate item in the 1950s to let him know when someone outside. In the front room was ping pong ball on a circular holder, high up a side wall. When the door was buzzed the ping pong ball, attached by a cotton string, would jump off the holder and swing along the wall, thereby attracting attention.

My Dad attended a school for the deaf, by train from London Bridge Station in Anerley south-east London, with other deaf kids his age. These kids stuck together and fought together through their teenage years against any piss-takers, and all remained friends. Those still alive came to my Dad's eightieth birthday party.

He left school and became a tailor's top presser in the East End, which he continued until he retired at sixty-three. One of his work mates was the singer Helen Shapiro's dad and another was the dad of Jazz musician Vic Ash.

My Dad became a hero in the deaf community in London when he represented Great Britain in the Olympic Games for the deaf in 1935, winning a gold, a silver and a bronze in the sprinting events. He told me that the British team got their own Union Jack made and sewn on their singlets as a sign of their pride in representing the deaf people of Great Britain.

After Dad's Olympic success he was asked to run for Blackheath Harriers, a top club, but there was a major drawback that hindered him furthering his sprinting career. In deaf athletics, the starter stood in front of the runners with a handkerchief above his head and dropped it to start the race. The hearing athletes had a starter with a gun, who stood behind the starting line. As my Dad's strength was a quick getaway, the starter gun didn't help him at all. So for the rest of his time, he competed with other deaf athletes quite successfully until middle age caught up with him.

Olympic Games for the Deaf 19 August 1935
Len Lewis at the start of the 100 yards race

Olympic Games for the Deaf 19 August 1935
Len Lewis is number four

22 | TALES FROM THE RANKS AND BEYOND

Len's team mates, White City 1935

Len Lewis' gold, silver and bronze medals won at the Olympic Games for the Deaf

Shortly before he died, the programme for the deaf, 'See, Hear' came to his flat, and he recounted his triumphs, which I have on video and treasure. At the peak of his athletic career, he looked like a film star: judge for yourself. At his eightieth birthday party his friends presented him with a cake with a runner on it.

He chased my Mum for a couple of years, but she wasn't interested for reasons that have been explained. Eventually, she went out with him for three years and they married at Shoreditch Registry Office. At the time of their passing, they had been married for sixty-five years.

From the time I could read, my Dad introduced me to his love of film and we made regular trips to the West End and foreign cinemas. I loved, and still do today, the French and Italian cinema, and the subtitles, especially the black and white ones. My Dad and I watched the classics. He could read the subtitles and, unlike when I relayed in sign language the plot of a TV film, I could relax and enjoy.

His knowledge of all films was astounding. We would watch an old black and white film on TV, and he would say, "The butler is _____" and the actor playing the butler would be a bit player, not the star. I would wait until the end of the film to see the credits. Sure enough, he was always spot on.

His love of cinema started when he was a kid and films had subtitles until the advent of the talkies with Al Jolson in 'The Jazz Singer'. My Grandad would give him the money to watch Charlie Chaplin and other silent movie stars. He told me he would sit in the cinema watching the whole show twice over.

He had a great love of anything he didn't have to hear: silent films, football, boxing, horse racing, the dogs, and his other great passion, athletics, which started when he attended a school for the deaf as a kid.

Later on, when he retired and TV started to have subtitles, he would get his weekly planning magazines and mark all the shows that had words. What a breakthrough for deaf people who wanted to enjoy TV in the same way as hearing people.

My Mother

Amy May Rogers was born on October 27, 1916 and she was a character. She was one of four children, three girls and a boy. The three girls were named after my Grandmother's sisters. She went deaf through whooping cough when she was eight years old and spoke with the accent that hard of hearing people have. She could have had a hearing aid but out of love for my Dad she said it wouldn't be fair to the Old Man. My Mum spoke with the memory of an eight year old. An example would be "Oh, I have known her for dog-end years".

"No, Mum, it's donkey's years" I would say. She never took any notice, so dog-end years it remained.

When we were looking at an insurance policy and we couldn't read the small print, she said to me "get your father's magnificent glass out".

We all laughed with my Mum, but never at her. She was a real firebrand from the toughest part of the East End, a place called Hoxton, where incidentally, the infamous Kray Twins were born.

My Mum kept up the toughness that she had been brought up with, except with me and her Grand-kids. When she was a kid of twelve, my Grandad Rogers would send her out to fight kids that hit her younger brother Percy. Most kids did not relish taking her on with a lump of wood in her hand.

Hoxton was almost lawless with an almost inbred disdain for the authorities. So much so, that the police patrolled in threes after one of their number was put head first down a manhole cover. The Hoxton gang was a forerunner to the Twins, and my Grandad Rogers had been a part of it. My Mum's Uncle Charlie - who fought in World War I and whose face was badly scarred - did eight years for biting a policeman's ear off.

I remember buying my Mum a box of chocolates, and when she opened them, they were off. She asked me where I got them. Then she went out and was back within twenty minutes, the box replaced, but not before she had made the shopkeeper open them in front of shop full of people. She came back and said "fucker cheek trying to cheat you". It didn't matter how many times you told her the word was 'fucking' she still said the wrong word.

Another gem was "there is a good film on the telly tonight."

"Who's in it, Mum?" I would say.

"East Clintwood" she replied.

When I was small, my Mum would come out of the flat at regular intervals to check on me and to ask, "who are you playing with?" If there were four other kids she would come back with freshly made chips for four, wrapped in a cone made of newspaper. All games ceased while we put salt and vinegar on our chips. After scoffing them down, activities resumed.

When I was ten my Parents bought me a record player, and we enjoyed a black and white television, and long before subtitles we would all sit round it. They would look at the screen and then turn to me for translation, so I would keep my eyes on the screen and do sign language for them: 'he said, she said'.

A stronger character than my Mum you couldn't meet, and if she didn't want to do something you couldn't persuade her otherwise. The following story highlights my Mother's strong will power. After she had another heart attack, I insisted in agreement with a hospital doctor that she should stay in for a couple of days for a check-up in hospital. I had Dad on the first floor and Mum on the second floor. After seeing them safely in their beds for the night, I got a cab back to the flat. As it was a one bedroom flat my bed was on the floor and made up with the three-piece suite cushions. About 8:30am I heard a key going into the lock and jumped up to see my Mum trying to get in. "I was not stopping there," she said. "So I got out and caught a bus," she continued. I couldn't work out how she got past the nurses undetected and the coded door on the hospital ward. I had given the hospital my mobile phone number, as I was next of kin, but the first phone call I received was from the police notifying me that "Mrs Lewis is missing from the hospital". The second call was from a Jamaican ward sister who informed me that "your mother has absconded". The final call was from the matron of Lewisham Hospital apologising for Mrs Lewis' disappearance. After telling them that she was safe with me at home I phoned my Son who cracked up with laughter and started in with the theme tune from 'The Great Escape'. She never did get those tests done.

My Parents were the happiest couple I've ever seen: he loved her and it was reciprocated although she didn't always show it. Even today, years after my Parents passed on, I sit and smile at their approach to life. With a little gesture in a crowded pub, my Dad would make me smile and I would know what he was talking about. He would pick out the characteristics of an individual in the pub by signing. It was our private world that couldn't be detected by anybody who wasn't deaf and who didn't know sign language. My Mum would sign to me to illustrate her annoyance at a nosey neighbour, but while signing she would be smiling, so nobody saw her true feelings, not that she was afraid of showing them.

In all the sixty-two years I knew my parents, I never wanted them to change. They had special qualities, as did their friends, all as open as a book. What you saw was what you got. Their world was never dull.

They travelled all over Europe. Even before the Brits invaded Spain, they had travelled to Italy, Spain, Switzerland and Austria.

One story about their travels abroad springs to mind. The greatest thing for a deaf person was to meet a hearing person who tried to communicate by signs or lip reading. Their faces would light up and the hearing person would have a friend for life. They got on especially well with signs and actions when abroad with the animated Romans and Spaniards. A classic story was when they were in Rome and Mum was buying a handbag. The woman in the shop had tears in her eyes and called her husband from the back office. Within minutes, the Italian couple had kissed Mum and Dad and gave Mum the handbag free of charge.

The deaf and blind were always a topic of conversation between me and my parents. They both said that if they had a choice, they would choose deafness. I had a pal who said he have taken blindness because he loved music so much.

My Dad loved visual things and filled his life with all sports, anything he didn't have to hear. My Mum always told my Uncle Percy she would have liked to have heard my voice. Mum, if it is my singing voice, you didn't miss anything. When they went to the deaf club, they enjoyed bingo (the letters lit up on a board), darts and snooker. But above all, they enjoyed the company of other deaf people: I've never seen so many happy people together.

The only time I was angry that my Parents couldn't hear was when we had a day out at Ramsgate. There were about four deaf couples with their kids. I was decked out in a knitted pair of swimming trunks that my Mum had made and which grew longer when wet. The beach was crowded and somehow I got lost. I was about five years old and someone took me to the lost children's rescue post where a loudspeaker announced the names of missing kids. All the deaf party searched the beach for me, hoping I hadn't gone into the sea. I was at the 'come and get me post' with two candles hanging down from my nose, telling the nurse that my Mum and Dad couldn't hear, so they wouldn't be coming for me. Luckily, a man using his best communication skills, told my Dad about the loudspeaker and where to go. When he arrived, I tried to kick him but he was as angry with me for getting lost. He put me on his shoulders with an ice cream, which dropped down his chest, and returned to the team of searchers. I remained 'in sight' until it was time for the train home.

For the rest of my life I never got angry because of their deafness and wouldn't have wanted to change them for the world. They were the best parents anyone could wish for.

Unfortunately, there was a lot of ignorance from people mocking and making gestures with their hands, and I sometimes took the wrong path with violence instead of feeling pity for the morons who should have known better.

Amongst the community in south-east London there were a group of young deaf men who were feared because people did not know how to communicate with them. They had the unfortunate nickname of 'the Dummies' and were a couple of years older than me. Whenever I went to a dance hall, they would call me over and ask how my Dad was. I spoke in sign language and a lot of people thought I was deaf, leaving me alone at the time, free from any bother as they feared my 'backup'.

My Mum and Dad's wedding day, south London meets the East End (above)

Dad (centre) with fellow Old Kent Road Deaf School pals in 1929, Fred Corp (left) and Don Caliendo (right)

TALES FROM THE RANKS AND BEYOND | 33

*London Select Deaf Team on the way to play
Brighton Deaf at football, 1930s*

34 | TALES FROM THE RANKS AND BEYOND

Gran and Grandad Rogers, who lived with us

Mum and Dad, Boxing Day, 1938

Dad at the races, looking like Fredo Corleone

TALES FROM THE RANKS AND BEYOND | 37

My favourite photograph, at the deaf club's Christmas party, 1951

Len Lewis on the day he left school, 1932 (left)

Dad asked if I would play in a cup final for the deaf football team, which I was delighted to do. As a ringer, I was told not to call names for the ball, but just to hold up a hand when you wanted a pass. This was difficult as anyone who knows me would say if was near impossible for me to shut my mouth for ninety minutes. However, the game went well: I got two goals and the team won the cup. The Old Man was over the moon and I had made some good pals in the deaf community.

South-East End Childhood

The conditions we lived in above the rag and bone shop left a lot to be desired but at the time beggars could not be choosers. There was one bedroom for my parents and I slept in the front room over the shop. My mother made a cover for my bed that matched the curtains so that when we had visitors it looked okay.

One summer's night I was lying in bed trying to get to sleep and all I could hear was the glass ashtray in the fireplace clinking against the tiles. In the half-light, I looked at the fireplace and could see about ten mice that had come up from the chimney downstairs.

I got up and woke the Old Man. We put a heavy piece of wood over the hole that the 'Great Escapees' came up from. The next day my dad bought mouse traps and left the piece of wood in place - that seemed to do the business.

On a larger scale of wildlife, we could see rats scurrying about on top of the tarpaulin from our dining area where we were eating. Always save the best until last.

In my Mum's kitchen was a cooker, a washbasin, and a toilet. When we moved in the toilet was not boxed in and my Dad got the job done by a pal. It was next to a window so that we had working air conditioning!

So, get the scene: all in a twelve foot by eight foot room, my Mum was cooking, my Dad was at the basin washing and I was having a 'Nelson Riddle'.

After the war, Gran Rogers lived with us in a council house. When I got out of bed and washed before going to my primary school, she would comb my hair with the then fashionable side parting. I had a cow's lick at the back of my head that wouldn't lie down until my Gran went to the frying pan and took some cooking fat. She rubbed her fingers with the fat and plastered the cow's lick and then off I went to school smelling of last night's sausages and onions.

As my Mum was working, it was left to Gran to educate me on the basics. I cleaned my teeth with salt and saw my Grandad use soot for his teeth. She taught me how to use my knife, fork and how to drink from a cup. You might think what's so hard about drinking from a cup? It was when you witnessed your Grandad drinking (slurping!) from the saucer. At bedtime, she would put the men's overcoats on my bed, which were retrieved for work the following day.

Gran Rogers lived with us until she died. I was her favourite grandson.

When I was suited and booted, and ready to go out for a jolly up, my Mum would tell me to go over to the pub and treat my Gran to a drink. When I walked in, she was with her old pals, Maude and Kitty.

Looking for a drink they would say, "Ain't he 'andsome, Ead."

"Okay girls, what you having?"

"I'll have a double rum," said Maude.

"No, you won't. Get her a single, Son. Same for Kitty and a Guinness for me," said Gran.

Their sessions were famous, and I always thought they were entitled to anything they wanted after two world wars and helping the younger women in labour while the Hun was bombing. Maude had bandy legs and her favourite line was "Lend me a half crown until me legs go straight." Those old gals could drink. I remember taking my Mum and Gran for a Mother's Day drink, and I think Gran drank about fourteen pints of Guinness, and then went home to cook dinner!

When she was in her eighties, Gran had a heart problem and was waiting for a pacemaker to be fitted. The day she died the letter for the appointment came through the letterbox.

My Parents went to the public baths where you paid for a bath. Unfortunately, when they were in their separate cubicles they couldn't shout out like the other bathers "More hot in number three" or "More cold in number seven" for the attendant to adjust. So they either got out of the bath, opened the door and caught the attendant's eye and made him understand more hot or cold water, or suffered in silence.

If two or more pals went to the baths it was a common practice to call out your mate's cubicle number with

"More hot in number six" which would be followed by an anguished cry from number six and a "Fuck you, Jimmy". Then, if Jimmy's number was known: "More cold in number ten" and so on, until the attendant threatened to evict both the offending parties. Happy Days!

Later on, I went to the Bradfield's Boys Club in Peckham and played five a side, table tennis and basketball. But more importantly, I always had a shower five nights a week. On Saturdays and Sundays after the match, we washed in a cold water trough in freezing conditions on park pitches.

Local hard men and gangsters would employ some of the tougher deaf men who were fearless to do their dirty work. My Dad knew four people that fitted into that category. Two were good friends and two were acquaintances. My Mum wouldn't let the latter into the house, as they were really dangerous and wanted my Dad as a 'tic tac man' at which he was adroit. They worked for the race track gangs as heavies and had the 'tramlines' on their 'boat races'. I was always pleased to see them, as they tossed me a half a crown and I studied their attire, which was always immaculate. The other two, my Dad's pals, were charming to their friends.

One of the Old Man's friends was Big Ernie P. He came from a big family in Deptford, and his entire family, parents and five children, were all deaf. Big Ernie was about six foot four and always wore a big trilby hat. My Dad's favourite story about him was when they were in their twenties and went 'up West' to this restaurant, ordering T-bone steak, chips, tomatoes and onions. At almost the last bite, Ernie spied a dead fly under a chip and called for the waiter. He became very animated, pointing to the fly and frightening the waiter. The manager, not wanting a scene in his nice restaurant in front of the other diners, calmed the situation and refused any payment for the meal. Dad smiled when he told me that Big Ernie had produced a matchbox from his pocket with a dead fly in it!

The other good friend was Frank H. He and his wife, Christy, were regular visitors to our flat. Frank was a regular at the Peckham billiard hall in Rye Lane, where he was willing to do a day's work for all comers, anywhere, anytime, as long as the 'greengages' were right. Frank was a man with film star looks: well dressed, very clever, with connections to the 'faces' in southeast London. He never bragged about the scores of jobs he had been on. I can't remember him ever being short of 'nelson eddies' or ever being employed in all the forty years I knew him.

Other deaf friends of my Parents had their own businesses. Rose Barratt was a successful dressmaker, making clothes for both the deaf and hearing communities. Her husband, a Popeye lookalike, was a docker and a great character. Arthur Prior had his own cobbler's shop in Kennington and another deaf friend had a stall in an East End market - all remarkable because their deafness was not a barrier to them.

When my parents were about to celebrate their sixtieth wedding anniversary on 24 December 1999, I wrote to the Palace, knowing that the Queen would send a congratulatory card, and asked for the communication to be sent my address in Scotland since my Parents spent Christmas with Pat and I in Scotland. The Palace duly obliged. A beautiful card with a picture of Her Majesty arrived, together with a nice note. The card was treasured, and after Christmas dinner, the Old Man said with a wry smile on his face, "I'd like to see the Queen's speech. Get the subtitles on, Son. I bet she mentions us." My Mum smiled and looked at me.

"Dollop," she laughed.

I have vivid memories of the family's drinking in a pub next to the canal in Queensbridge Road, Shoreditch. I would be outside the pub with young Kenny, a distant cousin, and my

Dad would come out to check on us and ply us with crisps and lemonade. We waited for what was a regular event every Saturday night: the pub door would burst open and two animated men, usually wearing big hats, would square up. Very quickly a crowd would form a circle and the two knocked seven kinds of shit out of each other, until one had had enough or someone stopped it. What bothered me was that the pub was just a few yards from the canal and me and Kenny expected someone to be knocked into the water. It wasn't that maybe they couldn't swim; it was more that the canal had dead cats and turds floating in it.

Whenever I came in battered my Grandad Rogers would say "out you go" despite Jimmy Ennis being two years older and a foot taller. I always went out fighting dirty to no avail. His arms were longer and kept me at bay until he could bash me hard.

From about the time I was fourteen, my Grandad had this obsession with measuring my height. When he was convinced I had stopped growing, he called excitedly to my Gran, "Ead, he's stopped growing! Thank fuck for that, he's only five foot seven." My Gran knew why he was pleased, although I, in my naivety didn't, and asked why my Grandad was so pleased.

"You can never be a copper unless you are five foot eight."

Grandad Rogers idolised his wife. She always kept a civil tongue in front of other people, but could never resist being cheeky in private. One day, Grandad said to me, "Course, boy, I seen him."

"Who, Grandad?"

"The Ripper," he said. "He had a case and was dressed in a cape and was in Spitalfields." This was a standard newspaper description.

My Gran was standing behind him and mouthed the words to me, "Fucking liar."

My Grandad kept chickens in our back yard, mainly for the fresh eggs for our breakfast. I remember feeding and watering them, and treating them as pets until one Christmas when I was about six years old. Turkeys were a little bit out of the family's pocket, so Grandad went out to do the dirty deed of wringing the neck of the fattest bird. He brought the chicken into the scullery and my Mum began to pluck the feathers in preparation for our Christmas dinner. Suddenly, the chicken, hanging upside down supposedly with its neck wrung, jumped off the table and ran around the floor bumping into everything. To this day, I cannot forget the scene. My Mum fainted and my old Gran slumped into a chair, calling for water. My Dad and Grandad chased the chicken into the yard where a second execution took place. The women revived and I refused to eat any Christmas lunch. Sixty six years later I seldom eat chicken.

In the forties and fifties there were always big families, usually three brothers and 'two skin and blisters'. Normally two of the brothers were okay people but if the third one was violent the other two closed ranks as a formidable trio. Families openly fought each other and carried grudges. So, as an only child I tended to hang with families I knew who would assist me if requested. The toughest parts of London were surrounding the Docks in the east or south-east, the Thames being the divider between these areas. There was no love lost between the two sides and I had split loyalties.

My Mum's family came from north of Tower Bridge, the East End, and my Dad from a mile south of the Bridge. The locals called it 'going over the water' whenever crossing over to one side or the other. As kids in the summer, we were taken to the north side of the Thames where there was a small beach for picnics. Not much swimming though, as the Thames was a bit 'one hundred to thirty'.

As a kid on Saturday I was taken down to the Den, home to the infamous Millwall Football Club. I was six in 1948 and my love for Millwall FC continues to this day. On Sunday mornings my Dad would take me to see his Mum and Dad. When I was the right age, my Dad, Grandad Nat and I drank in The Enterprise pub. To encourage more drinking, the landlord laid on olives, peanuts, anchovies, pickled herrings and gherkins – all free of charge. This 'guvnor' was a great character, with gold teeth, a diamond ring on his pinkie and a Churchill Cuban cigar in his mouth. I think this is where I picked up the habit of liking good cigars which I have enjoyed from the age of nineteen to the present day. My Dad rolled up with liquorish papers and Grandad Nat smoked woodbines untipped.

Both Dad and Grandad were always well-dressed and had a tailor at the Elephant and Castle called Levy's which is where I first heard the expression 'the full Monty'. This expression came from Sir Montague Maurice Burton, who founded Burton's tailors, and it meant 'suit, waistcoat, and the whole she-bang'. On the day after his wedding my Dad couldn't move his neck. On close examination of his wedding shirt he discovered he hadn't removed the cardboard from the collar. My Mum quoted her favourite expression: "Dollop"!

He Can't Speak Properly

After returning from the country at the end of World War II, my mother took me to the doctor's with a minor ailment. My mother communicated in signs and her hard of hearing speech. The doctor spoke to me and I replied in the same manner as my Mum. The doctor pronounced, "He can't speak properly. I think he is deaf."

When deaf couples have children, one of the first things they do is to stand behind the baby and either clap their hands or make a bang to see the child's reaction. So my mother felt that the doctor had insulted her intelligence as a caring parent. My Mum was infuriated and said, "Of course he isn't deaf", and pulled a toy dog from her bag and, without signs, said to me, "What's this?"

I replied as quick as you like, "A dog." So it was confirmed that I could hear but couldn't speak properly. It wasn't the last time I was told that. Four times in my life I have been told I couldn't speak properly, the last time being when I was in my late forties. After all my time in the country, away from the bombs, I had acquired my Mum's accent that hard of hearing people have.

Mum and me away from the Blitz in Farnham, Surrey, 1943

Teddy the Ted

When I was thirteen, my Dad's brother-in-law, my Uncle Sid, who owned the rag and bone shop where we lived, asked me to go to work for him on Saturday mornings. He was a kind man and paid me ten shillings for the day. I took the job, but only in the summer months when there weren't any football matches. I went out on deliveries with Teddy Waller who was about nineteen and a fully fledged Teddy Boy. Uncle Sid supplied fish and butchers' shops with white paper that was used to wrap up their goods. Teddy drove the Bedford van and I was his assistant. We got the rounds done in double quick time and then Teddy took me to a jukebox cafe where his pals, the Brockley boys, hung out.

At this time, in 1955, there were only the Teds or the bohemian traditional jazz cats, like beatniks. Every area in London bragged its own Ted gang and there were running battles between the various manors. All this added to the excitement of being in the cafe. I was more interested in the music of the day and my tea and bacon roll. Teddy vouched for me and adopted a big brother role and I never came to any harm.

I remember Teddy telling me that when the Deptford boys came calling, with bicycle chains and various weapons, they were led by none other than Chopper Green, (mentioned later in the book) of bug hutch fame and fearsome reputation.

About four years later, I used to walk a lovely blonde home from the Peckham Co-op Dance Hall. She was a friend who lived local to me and was a couple of years older than I was. She became Mrs Teddy Waller.

Don't Look Down

Shortly after starting grammar school, I was playing inter-house football, yellows versus blues, when it was noticed that the back of my shirt had blood on it. A teacher got an ambulance and I was taken to Lewisham Hospital where I was operated on within twenty four hours. Apparently, I had a nevus that had been growing on my back and had gone from my side almost to my spine. The scar from the initial operation was pencil thin, but as I grew it spread to about half an inch.

I went on to have radium treatment at Lambeth Hospital, Elephant and Castle, and I remember my Gran Rogers taking me on a train; we had to pass the Rowton House

Doss House in Churchyard Row - which Gran renamed Spital Alley, as the inhabitants had a habit of coming out to clear their chests. It was always a topic of conversation on hospital days. "Gran, can we go another way, please?" I would say.

"Not possible, Boy – head up, try not to breathe in." She was a tough old girl, with a heart of gold.

All my life I have been plagued by black moles on my back, and when I go out in the sun only my face, arms and legs get access to the rays. Better safe than sorry.

The Strangler

I recall that the milkman had a horse to pull his cart, and people came out with shovels to collect the manure for their gardens. We played football in the road at a time when a car was rarity to be seen. The girls played skipping and tucked their skirts up in their 'Alan Whickers'. We picked teams for football and the two captains chose alternate players; usually the last to be selected had glasses or were heavyweights. An Italian ice cream man came round on a bicycle with a box on the front and sold Italian lemon ice with bits of lemon sticking out.

One day a young couple were having a domestic in their kitchen, and she threw a frying pan at him. The frying pan ended up in the garden. After several minutes no one came out to retrieve it and all was quiet in the house. Probably, they were making up. So I jumped the privet and took the frying pan home for my Mum.

I was about six years old and walking home from school when a fourteen year old boy asked me for money. When he didn't get any, he tried to strangle me. He had a pair of National Health glasses with a plaster over one eye, blonde hair and one or two missing teeth. I recall that he was a bit backward and I knew where he lived.

Grandad Rogers always avoided the police and never grassed anyone to the authorities. My Dad, Grandad and I visited the boy's house and left it for his parents to sort it out, but not before my Dad shouted at the boy and was very animated. The boy was nonplussed, which indicated how bad his mental state was.

One of my pals was instructed by his mum never to get pally with a certain kid who was the son of a policeman in case he saw 'goodies' stashed in the backroom that were not exactly kosher!

The Blitz

When the War was over, there were stories about the Blitz, some sad, some funny, but mostly tragic. On 7 September 1940, about 5pm, 384 German bombers flew up the Thames and dropped their bombs on the people of south-east and east London, and the docks. At 7pm they went home. At 8pm 300 hundred more bombers came back. Among the casualties, a school at Keeton's Road, Bermondsey, took a direct hit. Thirty nine people died - including nineteen children - while seeking shelter from the bombs. It could have been worse: it was a Saturday and the school was closed. At the end of the first day of the Blitz, 650 people were killed and hundreds injured.

The saddest story I heard was of a man who searched the rubble in vain for his wife and seven children. He was completely mentally destroyed and never worked again.

My Parents lived in the bombers' target area, that is, the docks and surrounding districts. When they married, on 23 December 1939, the War had just begun, and they lived with my Mum's parents in Shoreditch. They were bombed out three times, living in different locations.

One night, returning from a visit to my Dad's parents, they were travelling back to Shoreditch, sitting upstairs on a number seventy eight bus that went via Tower Bridge, which was always raised during the bombing to prevent damage to a major connecting artery in London. Suddenly the air raid warnings sounded. The driver of the number seventy eight was almost at the point of no return on the bridge as it began to rise, and stopped just short of the abyss. Years later, my parents laughed about it, but not at the time.

When the bombs fell on Queensbridge Road, Shoreditch, my parents and Aunt Gracie (my Mum's sister) were in the shelter at the bottom of the garden. Their house took a direct hit and there was smoke everywhere. The Old Man put his head out of the shelter and was confronted by an air raid warden who was pulling him out. Peering through the smoke, my Mum thought the warden was a German and pulled my Dad back. As my Aunt told the story, my Dad went into the shelter five foot six and came out five foot eight.

One night in their flat in Stoke Newington, my parents and another deaf couple were playing Kalooki - a popular card game - completely unaware of the bombers overhead.

The bombs fell and the door to the flat fell on my Mum. Outside, in the underground shelter, people were gassed and drowned when a bomb made a direct hit. An elderly lady walked about, semi-conscious, with a large shard of glass in her eye. The next morning, in the forecourt of the flats, many bodies were covered with white sheets.

My Parents lived through these times, as did thousands of Londoners. At one time, the Germans bombed seventy six days and nights, with only one day's gap. Churchill stated, "Hitler doesn't know the fibre of Londoners. We will fight to the end."

London wasn't alone in being bombed. In May 1941, Hitler bombed major cities all over Great Britain. In Scotland, Clydebank had horrific carnage: only seven houses remained out of 8,000.

I, too, have memories. Of the doodlebugs, and the sound of their explosions, which have left me even today with a fear of loud bangs. Even the sound of fireworks causes me grief.

During the Blitz my family was bombed out three times. On one occasion, the Queen Mum came down to the East End the morning after a German raid. My Gran on my Mum's side was five foot tall and about sixteen stone. She stood in the frame of her front door and, as the Queen Mum approached, she curtsied. The Queen Mum asked where she lived and my Gran pointed to the bomb site behind her. The Queen Mum was visibly moved.

After I was born in 1942, my Mum, having lived through three bombings, took me away to Farnham, Surrey, joined by my Aunt Eadie and my three Cousins, Michael, Janet and Linda. Because of his deafness, my Dad was unable to join the armed forces but he remained in London, making uniforms. He came down to see us on weekends. At the end of the War, I was two and a half, and me and my Mum returned to London to live with my Dad, Mum's parents and my Mum's younger brother, Percy. Aunt Eadie stayed in Farnham and never returned to London, and I spent many a good summer holiday with my Cousins, running wild in the countryside, scrumping apples and swimming in rivers.

Uncle Percy
Uncle Percy saw it all: Dunkirk, D-Day and lost all his youth for six years. When I was older, he told me all the stories in graphic detail. He told me that after the D-Day landings, his squad was lying in a field in darkness and

TALES FROM THE RANKS AND BEYOND | 59

My Uncle Percy, who served from 1939 – 1945

could hear a clanking above them. His sergeant ordered him to climb up a tree to cut down the dead body of a British paratrooper, swinging lifeless.

After Dunkirk, Percy came home on leave and was afraid to go back to his unit after all the horrors he had seen. My Gran marched him down to Bethnal Green nick, winking at the desk sergeant that he was thinking of going AWOL. Uncle Percy did his duty to the end.

Percy was a good Uncle to me and taught me many things when I was growing up. Percy managed our football team, and we lost only one game in our first season, winning the league and cup. The team was called Club L after the Lyceum, our strip was styled after the Italian giants in Milan, AC and Inter. All the fellas were Mods from the Lyceum, and, despite my best efforts, the Lyceum wouldn't sponsor us, so we had a whip round amongst ourselves. I played at right back and was responsible for the kit, which in fact my Grandad washed and ironed every week. I designed two strips, perfectly suited for a team of poseurs. One was brown and black striped with brown shorts, with little numbers on the chest and matching brown and black socks, which was forward for the early sixties.

After the War

I returned from the country speaking the way my Mum spoke, with the accent that deaf people have, but it didn't last too long. By the time I started school, I was a voiceover for Grandad Rogers – a full-blown Cockney. And that's not surprising: I was with him for hours on end, hanging onto every word and story that fell from his mouth. All six of us lived in a three bedroom council house in SE6. I shared with Uncle Percy and it was good growing up in an extended family environment. My Dad worked in tailoring in the East End and my Mum worked in a brewery. Uncle Percy was in the Post Office, so we ate well. As my Grandad had been ill, he only worked here and there, so my two Grandparents looked after me all day.

Back in our home we had gas power and lighting, but before televisions were commonplace for the working class, we spent our evenings listening to the radio, or wireless as it was called, which was charged by batteries. One popular show, 'Educating Archie', revolved around a ventriloquist named Peter Brough and his dummy called Archie. Listeners enjoyed what they heard, and then the penny dropped: we were listening to a ventriloquist throwing his voice on radio, so how did we know how good he really was.

When Peter hit the stage, performing to a live audience, his career faltered. As the man said, you can fool some of the people all of the time and all of the people some of the time, but you can't fool all of the people all of the time!

On most Saturday nights, my Mum, Dad, Gran, Grandad and I would go 'over the water' from south-east to east London in a 'sandy'. My Gran's brother, Fat Sid, and his missus, Mary, were the landlords of a pub known as Little House, located opposite Repton Boxing Club. This was across the road from Vallance Road, where the Twins lived.

The pub had one small bar with a door at the end, leading to an upstairs apartment. Behind the door was Sid and Mary's kitchen and an old armchair with its stuffing coming out. This was where I would sit, as an eight year old, in the warmth of the kitchen, watching the mice, munching crisps and drinking lemonade. I would listen to singers, accompanied by a pianist, playing the old music hall tunes from times gone by. These were the songs sung by Harry Champion, Flanagan and Allen, Harry Lauder, and, most popular of all, Al Jolson with his songs of the Deep South and his mammy.

The pub is now housing. Rumour has it that before its demolition in the sixties, the Twins would ask Fat Sid to rent his pub for meetings of the Firm, as they knew it would be free of wiretaps or bugs, and that they paid for their use of the bar at the conclusion of their business.

Fat Sid and Mary were lovely people and both died in a nursing home when they were in their eighties. They never had any kids and I always got toys and sweets from them whenever I visited.

As I grew up, I always had divided loyalties between east and south-east London. My Mum's family were all East Enders, and my Dad's family were from 'across the water'. There was no love lost between the two areas. Young men courting a lady from the other side of his turf could find himself running the gauntlet, just trying to get home.

I loved my Mum's uncles and aunts. They were all Cockney characters, generous to a fault. I always got a 'Lord of the Manor' whenever I saw a family member, at the cost of having to endure a sloppy wet kiss from the aunts before getting payment. The men called me 'Boy', a term of endearment as in "All right, Boy, how ya going?" The best

I ever got was half an 'Oxford' from my Mum's Uncle Bert who was steaming and wouldn't remember having given it to me the next day.

Angels With Dirty Faces

After the War my Aunt Eadie and her husband Bob decided to stay in the Surrey countryside with my three cousins Michael, Linda and Janet. Every summer holiday I was taken down to Farnham to spend a couple of weeks running wild with Michael who was similar in age to me. It was a great adventure for an eight year old to swim in rivers, fish with a cane and bent pin, climb trees and go scrumping for apples and pears.

Up the hill where my aunt lived was a massive common with a burned out army tank, which was a meeting place for the local kids. All the kids were afraid of a man in his thirties called Reg, who unfortunately was not quite right in the head, and walked about with a big dog and a heavy walking stick. One day Michael spied Reg in the distance, walking in our direction on the common. He was petrified of both the man and his German shepherd. I suggested we climb a tree to hide. Reg walked by but the dog wouldn't stop barking at us stuck up in the top branch.

Michael was panicking because it was getting dark and past teatime. Losing his temper, Reg put the lead on the dog and stormed off, completely unaware of our presence. Giving it five minutes for man and dog to get ahead, we carefully made for home. I believe a few years later Reg was institutionalised.

I enjoyed some good times in the country but it all ended the day a policeman knocked at the door. Near to my summer residence there was a small park for the kids with a slide, swings and a see-saw. There was also a toilet in the park with a couple of traps, which I distinctly remember had green doors. Not happy with the playground amenities provided, Michael and I were swinging on one of the doors, on opposite sides. Needless to say, the door came off its hinges, and we both disappeared lively. The policeman who called was the local village Bobby. He came on his bicycle complete with clips around his ankles. He was red of face and spoke with a slight bur-r-r. Uncle Bob opened the door. I stood behind my Aunt Eadie, hiding. I knew what was coming.

"Have you got a boy from London stopping with you?"

Uncle Bob countered with, "Why? What's he done?"

"He's caused damage to the park's toilet."

"How do you know he's from London?"

"Two local boys gave evidence." Gave evidence!! By now I'm feeling like Al Capone and popped my head out from behind Aunt Eadie's skirt.

"It wasn't me," I said, shaking my head.

"Well, your accent is right and the two kids are willing to identify you."

This really was the big time, with both evidence and identity parade.

Uncle Bob said, "Go in the back room, Boy. I'll sort it out." He went down to the park with his tools and repaired the door. Michael never got cross-examined and I took the rap!!

When Mum and Dad came down to take me back to the Big Smoke, they were told the story and accepted my high-spirited behaviour without any punishment, other than it was best I didn't go back again. Who knows, they may have got Elliott Ness on my Daily.

When I met my cousin Michael later in life, at weddings and funerals, I always felt for him. Life didn't deal him the best of cards and he always told me that he wished his family had gone back to London with us after the War.

"You've had a great time in London. I've led a quiet life here in the country," he once told me. One thing for sure, I wouldn't have met the characters in a then sleepy backwater. But who's to say what's the better quality of life? To each his own.

****

Educating Roger

Elfrida Junior School

I don't recall anything too exciting when, at the age of five I went to Elfrida Junior School, a mixed school with both boys and girls. All the children of our neighbours went there. The girls wore bows and who had wonderful names like Deirdre, Erica and Penelope. The kids were all War babies and some of them had hang-ups because they had no socks, or had holes in their clothes, cardboard in their shoes to stop the rain soaking through or wore hand-me-downs from older siblings. Rationing was still on. My pal Derek, or Del, was always stealing Horlicks tablets from the chemist and dished them out to his cohorts who kept watch.

At junior school, there were several large poor families whose kids came to class in old work clothes and didn't always smell too good. Nevertheless, they had a good sense of humour, which can best be illustrated by the following story. There was this family with seven kids – five boys and two girls. The girls had one bed to share, but the five lads had to share three at the top and two at the bottom. Their ages ranged from four to ten, and not all of them were 'house-trained'. I remember one of the brothers telling me that their mum would ask, "What end to do you want to sleep?"

And the reply was "The shallow end, Mum." Another story of his was that his mum bought their clothes from the Army surplus shop, and that he was fourteen years old before he realised that he wasn't a Japanese soldier.

The boys wore grey trousers with a belt that had a snake clasp and sleeveless pullovers, knitted by our mothers, together with black plimsolls and a long-collared shirt, usually worn with one collar up in the air. Our hair was either greased down, parted in the middle, or side-parted, cut short back and sides usually by parents with a kitchen basin.

There was a kid in my class called Ray C, who was the envy of all the boys and wore a hand-me-down jacket from his older brother. Both pockets were filled to the brim with cigarette cards, which showed a sportsman with a big head and a little body, wearing his football or cricket strip, with all the details about the player overleaf. This was too much of a temptation for Derek H who constantly dipped into Ray's 'sky rockets'. Ray never missed them.

Ray's other claim to fame was that he lived in the same street as Sir Henry Cooper, beloved of every Cockney when 'Enery's 'ammer' put Cassius Clay on his 'bottle and glass'.

One of my teachers was Mr Roache, a nice man with a red face and who played piano at school assembly. I think that today he would have been pulled up for not being 'politically correct'. One of my earliest school memories was a joke he told.

"A black man was travelling in the no smoking compartment of a train. The guard came in, saw him smoking and prepared to write him a ticket for the offence. 'Ok, what's your name' he asked. The passenger looked at the window and said 'Nosmo King'".

Lots of kids didn't laugh, hence 'he who laughs last doesn't get the joke', but I did.

Mr Roache lived in a large house on Hayes Common in Kent, and one day he took the class to the countryside to see the wildlife and flowers. After the day out, he took us to his house and his wife gave us lemonade and cakes. This was a wonderful day for the ragged army.

I stayed at Elfrida until it was time to sit our eleven-plus exam, the results of which would determine my senior school education.

Grammar School

My Dad's private tuition paid off: I passed the eleven-plus exam and won a place to a grammar school. In the 1950s, there was a three tier system: grammar, central and secondary. Based on your eleven-plus scores, you were placed accordingly. Sadly, those at bottom of the pile, the secondary pupils, were taught lessons but were trained primarily for manual skills. I don't think there was any credence given to late developers.

I had a choice of three grammar schools: Aske, Colfe's and Addey and Stanhope. There was no competition for me since the first two played rugby and the latter football. The only downside of Addey and Stanhope, for me at aged eleven, was that it was a mixed school, something that a couple of years later became a benefit. There were kids from inner London and other, posher kids who lived in the suburbs and travelled in by train.

Addey and Stanhope Grammar School was in Deptford SE8, a tough working class area with generations of dockers with history going back to 1513 as a ship building area for what became the Royal Navy. The school song began with the lines "Hearts of oak that Deptford made guarded England well. The ships are gone but stands the school the shipwrights worth to tell." The school uniform was a brown blazer and cap with a silver badge. The girls had a blazer and a natty hat and wore brown 'Alan Whickers', required by school regulations and definite passion killers. The teachers wore gowns, and on special occasions the headmaster, Fred Tye, wore a mortar board hat.

On my first day, Grandad Rogers gave me his usual advice, "Don't let anyone take liberties."

The deaf community in London belonged to regional clubs and knew each other, so if a deaf parent's kid started at the school, they would all know about it. My Dad had a deaf pal whose son was in his last year at the school, and, as good as gold, sought me out at the gates and promised protection against the bullies. He was a kindred spirit with deaf parents and took the role of older brother. In my turn, if my Dad told me the child of deaf parents started school, I would try to educate him so he wouldn't encounter any surprises.

I was okay in my early days because of my Grandad's admonition to only 'go forward'. After a couple of scuffles, I was left alone. One such scuffle was on the eve of a heavyweight boxing match between the American champion Rocky Marciano and a London man, Don Cockle. The bully, a big bonky boy who could pass for a farm labourer, came dancing to the class, shadow boxing. He punched me on the back of the head saying, "I'm Don Cockle." I wrestled him on an open desk and smashed the lid on his head twice saying, "And I'm Rocky Marciano!" He threatened me that after school he would be waiting. I waited and like the heavyweight fight that evening, Don Cockle lost the day.

Looking back, with all the problems in the world caused by religion, I can honestly say I couldn't tell you the religion of my close pals at school. The only one in my school whose religion was recognisable was a Jewish boy who, on special occasions in the Jewish calendar, wore a skullcap. Nobody took liberties with him. The worst he got was a nickname of Doberman after a character in the TV series, 'Sergeant Bilko'. If anyone threatened him with violence, our little gang looked after him. There were about six of us who hung out together and watched each others' backs. One of our roles was to protect the little kids from any bullying.

This was unlike years later when I lived in Scotland, working in Glasgow, where it is of great importance to know what a chap's religious beliefs are, hence Rangers versus Celtic, or in other words Protestant versus Catholic. The following conversation actually took place:

Cab driver: "What school did you go to?" Fishing for a clue respecting religion, should said school contain 'St Something or Other'.

Me: "I went to Addey and Stanhope Grammar in Deptford south-east London." No clue given.

Cab driver: After a frustrated period where I am not coming across with the answers. "So what team in Glasgow do you support?"

Me: "Partick Thistle."

Cab driver: By now he has really run out of roundabout questions and decides to go for the kill. "What religion are you?" wanting a simple Catholic or Protestant.

Me: Despite not having a religion, "I am Jewish."

Cab driver: Not wanting to be beaten, "Is that a Catholic Jew or a Protestant Jew?"

Good Glasgow humour!

The toilets were underground in the boys' playground. It had three traps and a line for taking a 'nelson riddle'. One big boy called Parish delighted in frightening the little kids and clumping them around the head. The inevitable happened. I was in the playground with one of my pals playing football (with a tennis ball), when a first year kid came up to us crying because of Parish. We bided our time until the Big P went down to take a pee. We got him and put both of his arms behind his back, led him to one of the traps, pushed his head into the bowl and pulled the chain. We told him why we took the action and promised him more of the same if he continued in his bullying ways. I think he must've thought about it long and hard, but he desisted after that day.

In the mixed gender classes, I was placed in the top tier of two. I loved geography, history, French, English language and literature. I hated science, maths, Latin and musical education. I did well in the subjects I liked and, in the mock GCEs, I was top of the class in French, something that prompted the French teacher to say, "Lewis is the only boy that speaks French with a Cockney accent."

My dislike of certain subjects was akin to the distaste for the teachers who taught them. As an example, our music teacher was a brutal Welshman, Taffy Roberts, a quick-tempered man with quick fire hands who wore a flower in his buttonhole and had a vicious right-hand slap. One day he slapped Doberman around the head in front of the class and poor old Doberman cried. It was my turn next. I was about fourteen, and he asked me a question about Handel, who wasn't my subject; Buddy Holly or Bill Haley, maybe, but not Handel. He slapped me hard about the head, expecting me to cry. I smiled, which angered him even more.

"Get out of my sight! Stand outside the door!"

"Okay," I said, smiling but wanting to cry with the pain of a sore ear that ten years previously was tested for mastoids.

"Fuck him," I thought. "He ain't making me cry." And he never did.

Mr Pitman was another man handy with dishing out pain. He doubled at maths and physical education. I never liked him because he punished the weakest in the gym. If a boy couldn't climb the rope or do press ups, they got whacked with a plimsoll shoe across the 'Khyber Pass'. He entered me as our school's representative in the hundred yard dash event, competing with other schools, but I wanted to do the longer distance events as I had better stamina for these, and I told him so. He refused to listen and put me in detention where I had to write out lines for an hour after school; I soon mastered the two-pen system.

Pitman taught algebra and trigonometry, which I struggled to comprehend. When I took my homework home, I sat there despondent and none of the family could help. As there wasn't a phone in our house to call pals for help, I relied on a girl in my class who lived nearby and was always helpful. When she wasn't about, I got detention and more lines from Pitman. I think he resented me being school captain of the football team, which didn't come under his jurisdiction. When the headmaster would announce the school football results in Monday's assembly, and my name got mentioned, I would always crack a smile in Pitman's direction.

I got the option to drop Latin. As it was a dead language and I wasn't going to be a doctor or a chemist, I dropped classes.

About this time in 1956, I was into football and rock n roll. Ask me any team's home venue, what colours they played in or their nickname, and I'm your man. On the radio there was Elvis, Jerry Lee Lewis, Fats Domino, Little Richard and Chuck Berry, to name but a few. Teddy Boy gangs were everywhere. I had a Tony Curtis haircut with a ducktail at the back. So, imagine the sight: I went to school with my cap resting at the back of my head so as not to mess up the Tony Curtis, and even then never put it on until I was around the corner from the school, hoping that no staff members would clock me along the way.

I was never cheeky to the teachers, but if I was clumped or picked on, I showed dumb insolence, just sitting there with a stupid half smile on my face.

During football season, I ran a football pool every Friday. It was simple: all English teams were put into my school cap and for a tanner, all the kids, both boys and girls, picked a team out of the hat. I had a chart with all the teams and I put the kids' names against the team picked out. The winner was the kid whose team scored the most goals on Saturday. If two or three teams all scored five goals, the winner was the person whose team had the least goals against them. In the case of a draw, the winnings were split evenly. Of course, the winnings were distributed after my 10% commission. Everyone was happy: no one was forced into participation and no juniors (i.e. under thirteens) were allowed to play.

One day I was summoned to the headmaster's office. Fred Tye was a tall thin man and looked a little bit like Alastair Sim.

"Come in, Lewis."

"Yes, Sir."

"I hear you are the school bookmaker."

"Not on a grand scale, Sir," I continued.

"I won't have gambling in my school. Although I can possibly see you as an entrepreneur in a few years, you have to be punished."

"Yes, Sir" I said, fully expecting his reaction.

The school bookmaker

"Hands or backside?"

"Hands, Sir." Six whacks later I was back in class. End of extracurricular activities. Until next Friday.

A short while after the caning, it was open evening at the school. It was decided that as my Parents couldn't communicate with the teachers, my Grandparents would go in their place and discuss my progress. I knew my Grandad would put himself about and seek out the headmaster who might tell him about my William Hill activities. As the evening went on, the French teacher, Mr Smith, was glowing, the football coach, Digger Dawson likewise and Mr Pitman not so much. Then Grandad came across Fred Tye.

Good evening. I'm Roger Lewis' Grandfather and I'm a bit concerned that he's falling in with the wrong company."

Said Fred, "I'm sorry to tell you this: he is the wrong company!"

Grandad wanted more information but good ol' Fred was reluctant to drop me in it, and Gran Rogers, who always favoured me, gently ushered her husband away. When they went home, my Parents wanted to know every detail.

Grandad said, "Everyone said what a good boy he is."

Everybody was pleased. The Old Man went out and bought fish and chips for all, with pickled onions and cucumbers. When no one was about, Grandad winked at me and said, "Good boy." I think he saw something of himself in me.

About 1956, once a week, we paid to get into the junior dance halls in the evenings. The dance halls were a meeting place for the fourteen to sixteen year olds – boys and girls – to eye up the local talent. The fashion for the girls was hooped skirts, which rose up when the girls leaned forwards, revealing stockings, suspenders and their 'Alan Whickers'. My pal, Ginger Fred, would pitch an old penny near the girls' feet, and the girls would all bend over, looking for what had dropped. The boys all kept straight faces and repeated the coin dropping a couple of times a night. Eventually, the girls would suss out what was going on and wouldn't talk to any of us, calling us names like 'pervert' or 'disgusting pigs'. We used to wind them up by saying that their knickers were an improvement on the brown school issue ones.

I suppose Deirdre was my first 'Richard the Third'. She told her pals I was her boyfriend. Her dad owned a greengrocer's. I walked Deirdre home from school, but whether it was because I was a gentleman at the age of eight or because she told her dad to give me an apple is debatable.

Back in school, Fred Tye retired, replaced by the most fearsome headmistress, who was also my English teacher. She had a face only a mother could love, and she ruled with an iron fist. Compared with her, Fred was a lamb. When it came to the cane, she called in a muscular teacher to administer punishment. A case in point was my pal, Brian, who took a day off from school.

It was customary for your mother to write a sick note when you returned to school, only in this instance, Brian's younger brother, who was also at school, wrote the 'sick note'. The note arrived on the headmistress' desk, whereupon Brian's mother was summoned to her office. His mum denied all knowledge of the letter, as it stated 'I kept my son BRAIN away from school because of a heavy cold'. His mum went home. The two brothers were summoned to the headmistress' office and were given no options. I recall they had difficulty sitting down for a day or so.

I captained the under-twelves, under-fourteens and the first elevens in football. The captain took home the football on Friday nights in a net, ready for the Saturday game.

Back when I was eleven, all the kids wore football boots that covered the ankles in a coarse, tan leather that needed dubbing to keep them supple. My Dad, who watched me play and was proud as punch that I was captain, took me to a sports shop and bought me a low cut, Continental-style pair of boots. I was the only kid in the school that had them, and physiologically they improved my game: I went on to get one of my only school prizes, my colours for football.

The other prize was a book, 'Great Expectations' that I won after the school was taken to see David Lean's film version, and I was awarded the prize for the best description of the film.

After Grammar School

When I left school and started to look at the world seriously, I began to pinch other people's clever sayings, but never using them in front of 'the donor'. It was just a part of character building.

I learned pub etiquette from Grandad Rogers. If you walked into a pub it was form to be bought a drink by your intended company. If the drink wasn't forthcoming, it meant one of two things. Either they were discussing business that was none of yours, or they didn't want your company. To be assured of good service, always buy the barman a drink, especially when the pub is mobbed. If you are sent a drink over from other company in the 'battle cruiser', always reciprocate. Above all, always stand your round and keep in turn. Best to remember who buys the round before you and then follow. In our company we had a guy who was slow in coming forward, which prompted the following comments:

"He's like a Scotsman with short arms and a long sporran." And when he finally put a note on the bar: "Fuck me, even the Queen blinked."

I never wanted to embarrass myself, so if I didn't have the cash, I wouldn't go out. If you ain't got no socks, you can't pull 'em up. I had silly sayings that I lived by.

"In this world no one is better than me. We are all born equal." I used this later in life at times when I was pitched up against more educated people. To make myself feel superior, I'd look at his shoes and think cheapo, shirt probably from Oxfam shop and white socks is he serious?

This was all behind an affable smile and I felt better than equal and ready to get down to talk.

My aspirations before I left school were to be a football reporter, anything to do with films or a tailor. In later life I think I could have been a football reporter, and whilst watching matches on Sky, I often pass comments that the commentators come out with after I've said them.

My greatest compliment about films came when I was at a soiree with six other couples. We were playing Trivial Pursuit, men versus the women. The men won and one of the women said, "We never had a chance with Barry Norman over there."

As for being a tailor, my Dad had the foresight to say that the handmade suit was going to be a thing for the chosen few. The rest were going to get off the peg cuts. He was 100% right.

Uncle Danny

When a Jewish person dies, a stone setting is held a year later. When my Grandfather Nat died, the stone setting took place at Waltham Abbey. My parents and I were at my Uncle Sid and Aunt Pat's house in Streatham with other family and friends for snacks and drinks. My Uncle Danny, who converted to Judaism, who was never a great fan of my mother or me because we never embraced the religion and felt my interest in trade unionism bordered on communism.

As the evening progressed, I was enjoying the company of my two cousins, Adrienne and Lindsay, two lovely girls. I was introduced to a very successful Irish businessman with the same last name as me, Sammy Lewis. He asked who my tailor was, how old I was, what I worked at, and did I speak French (which I did). About thirty minutes later, Uncle Danny asked to speak to me outside. Knowing his dislike of me, I expected some more rudeness or criticism. But no.

He said, "Sammy is interested in offering you a job. He wants you to open a factory for him in Paris and to run his business. Are you interested?"

Completely taken aback, I was a bit cagey and replied, "I need to know more. Salary, accommodation, holidays and any other fringe benefits."

Uncle Danny said, "Sammy is impressed with you and feels you could do a job of work for him. We can have a meeting early next week. We both, of course, will expect you to become Jewish."

Thinking that if I was a good prospect as a non-Jew, how would hours of study at a synagogue make me a better businessman? Having my principles, and noting the half smile on Uncle Danny's mouth, I was true to form.

"Tell him thanks, but no thanks."

I often think about being in 'Gay Pahree', but not the 'gay' part, the part where the mademoiselles come into play and where my life would have gone in Montmartre and les Hailles. Who knows? I may have liked wearing a beret and a striped jumper.

Heinemanns

I left school with 'O' levels in English literature and English language. On the strength of this, I got a job as an office boy with Heinemann's, an international publishing house, founded in 1890 by William Heinemann, in Covent Garden. My aim was to become involved in sports writing. While waiting for an opportunity to open up in the sports department, I worked in the basement with Jock the post room manager and a lad from a wealthy Indian family, who was also looking for a career in writing. In the meantime, I performed my duties with the post and delivered books to authors all around London. I met Bobby Charlton and Billy Wright, who was England football captain at the time.

The managing director was a Scot. He like the cut of my jib and took me into the sports department. The head man told me in no uncertain terms that I would need elocution classes before he would let me work in his department. I got the hump and thought it was written work that counted, not vocal. Later in the week, I was in the post room when the Indian chappie from the good background decided to take the 'Christopher Lee' about my accent. I thought he had taken a liberty, with him speaking like Peter Sellers as an Indian doctor in 'The Millionairess', the 1960s film with Sophia Loren based on the 1936 play written by George Bernard Shaw. One thing led to another, I gave him a right-hander and was promptly dismissed. Jock and the MD were sorry to see me go, and each slipped a fiver in my hand. My wage was four pounds, twelve shillings and six pence a week. It was 1959.

Great Expectations

If a boy had a police record as a juvenile, or had been to Borstal, options were sometimes limited, and he could follow a life of crime, which wasn't unknown in the east and south-east manors. The cab trade was always a popular choice for men. When the docks were closing, there was a great influx of men doing 'the Knowledge'. Likewise, the market workers who didn't fancy pulling their 'Sir John Barbirollis' when approaching their fifties, doing 'the Knowledge' on a part-time basis as there was no pay when you committed to 'getting on yer bike'.

One older cab driver told me that when he passed his degree at the London School of Economics, it was easier than doing the Knowledge. It was a statistic that only 40% saw it through and obtained the coveted green badge.

In the working class areas of London, the top aspirations of the young men were broken down into several categories:

The Docks – usually father-son tickets;

Cab Driver – use your gumption and go for it;

The Print – closed shop accessible through family connections;

Publican – first get some dough and then build on it;

Fruit, Meat, Fish Markets – recommendations;

Boxing – if you had it, you could make it;

Football – a working class game; to make it you had to be special and be noticed in junior football.

In working class areas, there was no 'silver spoon' syndrome where daddy introduced you to the Stock Exchange or took you into the family business, unless it was a butcher shop, fish and chip shop, scaffolding or fruit and veg enterprise. A lot of boys joined the Royal Mail as messenger boys and went on to become postmen, drove buses when of age and generally looked for steady work with a pension at the end of the day. The docks, markets and the print were all 'not what you know but who you know'. Boxing was a way out and the old adage 'the best fighter is a hungry fighter' was never so true. The working classes have thrown up world champions; I can't think of any from the upper classes. Football is a working man's game throughout the world. I had plenty of pals who made non-professional teams and got a tenner in their boots on a Saturday.

My only two pals that made professional football were Dave Metchick who played for Fulham with the great Johnny Haynes and Sir Bobby Robson in the 1960s. I have known David for fifty years. Today, he drives a London cab and is a genuinely nice man. The other is Dave Harper, who went to my school and played pro for Millwall and Ipswich. He became a cab driver and eventually a publican.

Another aspiration was to be a publican when the pub trade was good (before the smoking ban). Back in the sixties, the most successful publicans were ex-celebrities from the world of boxing or football. Every pub had its day as a popular venue because of having a good singer on at the weekends. My favourite singer was at the Green Gate in Bethnal Green. The blind singer, Lenny Peters - who went on to stardom - was a big attraction, as was Ginger Joe, a Smithfield meat porter who sang at The Vulcan on the Isle of Dogs, Millwall. The Twins were regulars at the Green Gate. Ronnie Kray would request songs from Lennie Peters, and, despite being blind, he would recognise Ronnie's voice from the crowd.

"Lennie."

"Yes, Ron."

"From Russia with Love."

There was no refusal.

Eventually, after my abbreviated foray into the world of publishing, doing a bit of 'this and that', I was recommended by friends to work at the Old Covent Garden fruit and veg market, before I embarked on my greatest career as a London cab driver.

Me and My Dad

When I passed the eleven-plus and won a place to grammar school, my relatives were amazed - something I didn't find out for sixty years. My Mum's younger sister, my Aunt Grace married a Canadian soldier during the war and emigrated to Canada. When my Mum died, I phoned her. During the phone, call she said, "We were all proud but amazed that you went to grammar school."

"Why amazed?" I asked.

"Well, because your parents were like they were."

I didn't take exception because she was elderly and because when she left for Canada I was just a baby. She didn't see the hours my Dad put in teaching me capital cities, arithmetic, spelling and reading. Because he couldn't speak or hear didn't mean he was backward - very far from it. He was a clever man, and I often wondered what he could have done with his life if he had had his hearing.

Below is a story he wrote, aged fourteen, published in his school magazine. I think he wrote it because he had a fear of water.

A Narrow Escape by L. Lewis (Totally Deaf)

Tom and Harry lived in Devon near the sea. One day they wanted to hunt crabs and find some shellfish. But their parents warned them that the tide came in swiftly. Tom and Harry defied their parents and they went over the rocks to the beach. On that fine day they paddled at low tide to look for the crabs. At last they began to feel hungry, so they took their lunch out of their bag and ate it. They said to each other that they wanted to sleep for a little while on the big rock. So they slept peacefully for one hour. To their surprise, when they woke up, they saw the sea all around the rock. It was now an island. The tide rose higher and higher, and they felt they were in danger of drowning. They began to cry (for they were only small boys). When two hours had passed, the water rose higher than ever, and it looked very dangerous for the boys, and they began to feel hungry again. Their parents had asked a boatman to search for their sons. At last the boatman found them, and the boys were so glad, but they were still crying. When they reached their home, their father scolded the boys. He said they must not disobey their parents from now on. After such a narrow escape, I don't think they ever did.

As his only child, he idolised me and I never let him down, and loved him unconditionally. From the time when I was sixteen, I always had my suits made and although I didn't ask, he cleaned my shoes and pressed my suits as he wanted me to look the part. Perhaps it was because we lived in a flat above a rag and bone shop. It didn't mean we had to be scruffy.

When I was about eight years old and playing in the streets with my pals, my Dad would be walking home from work at the same time as the ice cream van was ringing the chimes to sell us his wares. I would run up to my Dad and ask for the money to buy Italian ice cream from a little man who looked like Tony Curtis. He always played a little joke on my pals, via me, in sign language. If there were three of us, for example, he would say, "Tell them they can have an ice cream if they pass my spelling test." I was used to the joke and knew what was coming. He told me to ask Charlie to spell 'dog'. Okay. Then he asked me to spell 'cat'. Okay. Finally, he would ask Fred to spell 'Czechoslovakia'. After the laughter died down, he gave us the money. That was his sense of humour.

The only falling out we ever had in sixty-two years was totally my doing and he taught me a lesson. The lesson was that although he would give me the world, I must never disrespect him. I was about fourteen years old and James Dean was the big deal. I had faded jeans, white T-shirt and a black leather jacket always with the collar up. I had walked a young lady home and lost track of time. It was 11pm. As I crossed the road to the flat, my Dad was standing in the doorway of the downstairs shop. He was in his vest and trousers and wanted to go to bed. I had seen his temper but it had never been directed at me before.

"Where have you been?"

I was acting James Dean, the rebel without a cause.

"What's it got to do with you?" I said. Big mistake. He gave me a back hander across the face and said, "Get up them fucking stairs."

I didn't need telling twice.

The next day I apologised and disrespect in the family never happened again until thirty-one years later. My son, Daniel, was fourteen, had long hair, a leather trendy jacket and was out past his curfew.

"Where have you been?" I said.

"What's it got to do with you?" was the reply.

He got a back hander, and I lifted him by the collar of his jacket against a wall. He struggled.

"You ain't ready for me yet," I said.

"When will I be?" he asked.

"When I'm sixty five," I said. I've been looking over my shoulder for the past eight years!

Like the Boy Scouts' motto 'be prepared', my Dad was always prepared, just in case someone couldn't understand what he wanted. It wasn't easy for him to say "Holburn Viaduct, return please" at the ticket office, so he wrote it on the ubiquitous pieces of paper he carried in his pocket.

On the day Grandad Nat died, my Dad's sister, Lillie, phoned me at 7.30am to break the news and to ask me to tell my father, who had already left for work. I knew he took a number forty seven bus to London Bridge, so I jumped in the cab to chase the bus. I passed one number forty seven, parked the cab about half a mile along and got out to see if I could see him upstairs.

He was at the front, upstairs reading his paper. I caught the bus up at Surrey Docks and put the cab in front of it, explaining to the driver who was good about it. When I touched my Dad on the shoulder, I could see the fear in his eyes; he knew it was something terrible for me to be on the bus with him. We got off the bus and I moved the cab, thanking the bus driver.

I explained to my Dad in sign language. He broke down, and we stood in the early morning rush hour cuddling each other. I loved my Dad, and he loved his Dad, as I did. We all were close.

When my Dad was born in 1916, it wasn't unknown that profoundly deaf kids were put into asylums, being diagnosed as being somewhat retarded. My Father had no such fears with his parents, who doted on him and gave him the best of everything. He was a model son visiting his parents up to three times a week. He gave me good advice for life: "You have got two best friends in life – your mother and your money. Look after them both."

The Sporting Life

When I was in my early teens, my Dad would take me to the boxing halls such as York Hall in Bethnal Green or Manor Place, Walworth. If it was a good bout, the crowd would throw money into the ring for the boxers. This was called nobbins. But this was not always the case.

The Old Man was always shrewd, and could sense trouble. One night at Manor Place Baths, the local boy was going to lose. The natives were getting restless. My Dad told me to go to the back of the hall, and sure enough, when the decision came, chairs were thrown from all directions into the ring as punch ups erupted between the different sets of supporters.

After the fights, my Dad would take me to a stall, just off the Old Kent Road, that sold pease pudding, faggots, savaloys and chips, covered in onion vinegar, all for the outrageous price of one shilling.

Wrestling was big in the fifties and sixties, and we would go to Camberwell Baths to watch moody bouts where heavy blows were mock delivered, guys getting thrown out of the ring with not a drop of claret to be seen. Then, as now, people see it as a form of entertainment.

My Dad and Uncle Percy loved the greyhounds. One night at Wimbledon they won £600, which was a lot of money in the late 1940s. They came home with fish and chips for all, claiming to have found a fool proof system, which was put to the test a week later at Catford. They came home having returned the £600 to the 'poor' bookies.

One Saturday afternoon when Millwall were playing away and I was at a loose end with a wage packet in my 'sky', I asked my Dad if I could go with him to an afternoon meeting of the Charlton dogs. I could sense that he wasn't keen on me going. The inevitable happened: not a single winner and all my 'greengages' lost. He never gave me any advice on tips or favourites; he just stood there with a wry smile. It was something he didn't want for me. He had seen his dad lose fortunes and wanted me to learn a lesson. On the way home, I asked him to lend me a couple of quid so I could go out that night. A refusal. A knockback. This was the man who would have given me anything within his powers, but he wanted to teach me a lesson. He was a Spieler as his Dad had been before him, and as far as he was concerned he wasn't going to let that become a way of life for me.

I learned my lesson and don't go to the dogs. I bet on football and boxing in moderation – a two horse race – and perhaps once a year go to the races for a nice day out. Betting definitely has not gotten a hold of me.

****

It was a bad time for the family.

Dad had been in the hospital for a couple of months and wasn't able to function properly. Meanwhile, my Mum was having heart attacks and was very vulnerable in the flat alone. I was in Scotland and every Friday took the first flight to London, coming back on the last flight Sunday evening. During the week, Janet, my first wife, went to the hospital with my Mum and made sure she was fed and looked after, for which I was grateful. My Son and Daughter played their part, but it was down to me to make the final decision as what was best for my Parents.

After three months, the hospital wanted my Dad out for the bed space, but he needed care that my Mum wasn't physically able to give because of her heart condition. I hadn't had a weekend at home for three months, with each trip to London costing an average of £300, including travel and refilling my mother's fridge. I would have willingly spent £3,000 a weekend if they were together again and happy. I needed them to be close to me where I could see them every day. I wanted their last times to be dignified and happy.

I applied to the only deaf care home in Scotland, which was about an hour's drive from my flat. The place would have been perfect; all the people there were deaf and friendly. The lady who ran the care home was lovely, but unfortunately, could not take my Dad because he was bedridden. She was willing to take my Mum, but separating them after sixty five years of marriage was not on. The hospital in London had made it clear that my Dad had to go elsewhere, but I wasn't prepared to split them up. It was the last thing my Mum or I would have done.

After visiting several nursing homes, Pat and I came across the Orbiston Nursing Home in Motherwell, which was a five-minute drive from us. Lewisham Hospital kindly had my Dad transported to Scotland in an ambulance and my Mum went with him.

My Dad was not compos mentis, and he was losing a lot of weight. My Mum's short term memory was fading quickly and she was also losing weight. Both were eighty eight years old.

We told Mum that going to Scotland was a break for them, and she was only too happy to have her husband back. I kept their flat on and paid the rent. The neighbours kept an eye open.

At the nursing home, my Parents had a double room. The staff were good to them but were unable to converse, and waited until I came in the evening to explain what was happening with medication and other day-to-day activities.

When Pat and I visited every evening, my Mum would rush at me, asking when they could go home. This became the norm on every visit and she wouldn't let it go. I was getting uptight, knowing they couldn't look after each other any longer. So my reply to her request was, "Okay, get packed."

"What about your Dad?" she asked.

"He can't go. He's not well enough."

"Okay, then I'll stay," she acquiesced.

This happened every night because Mum couldn't remember the previous night's conversation.

We took them their favourite sweets, biscuits and newspapers, and tried to make them as comfortable as possible. The nursing home was wonderful to them. I think the nursing home went that bit further because of their deafness.

At Christmas, I was allowed to bring them to the flat for lunch although the sister at the nursing home wasn't keen, as she felt they might become disoriented away from their new home. My Son-in-Law, Liam, a big strong handsome specimen of Scottish manhood, carried my Dad from his wheelchair with a fireman's lift over his shoulder up fifteen stairs to an armchair. So my Mum and Dad had a good last Christmas with the people who loved them. After Christmas lunch, Mum entered the women's team for 'Who Wants to be a Millionaire', and to my amazement, she answered several questions correctly. Not amazed that she knew the answers, but that, given her loss of short term memory, she could still focus.

One morning, at 10.30am, I had a phone call from the nursing home to ask me to come there. After refusing to tell me why at first, the sister finally told me the worst: my mother had died.

The previous night we had visited the nursing home and I noticed that Mum wasn't well. She told me to look after Pat and myself. She didn't walk with us out to the door as she usually did. I spoke to the sister and she had noticed a change with Mum and said she would monitor her.

I got a cab from my office in Edinburgh to Motherwell, and found Pat and my two Step-daughters, Shonna and Cherelle, all in the room with my Mother. Nobody had told my Father, and he was with the other patients, sitting around the television. The sister asked me to tell him. I wheeled him into the room and he asked me, "Where's Mummy?" I pointed to the bed where she was lying. He kissed her and we all cuddled him.

The saddest day of my life: my Father had lost his best pal of sixty five years and I had lost my lovely Mum.

My Dad lasted two months after my Mum passed on. He just gave up. He told me he wanted to go to sleep and he did just that. On Adolf Hitler's birthday, he passed away. Ironic, given the hatred felt for Adolf.

Pat and I had left his bedside at midnight after a doctor told us it could be any time in the next twenty-four hours, and advised us to go home and get some sleep. At 1.00am, we got the call and went back to say our goodbyes. I don't think my old Dad could have weighed more than five stone at the end. Standing all day in his job had given him varicose veins in both legs so that he had to wear elastic stockings, but he still never had a line on his face and still had a full head of hair.

I remember our last lucid conversation and telling him a white lie. My Dad was from Bermondsey and a Millwall fanatic. He asked me their result on the previous Saturday (they lost at Derby County 0–1), but I told him they had won 1–0. He smiled, gave me the thumbs up and went to sleep forever. I lost my best pal, a man that I loved and reciprocated that love tenfold over. He gave me all his love and kindness and was proud of me, as I was of him. He was eighty eight.

From the Mouth of Babes

I love all kids and old people. All those in the middle I need to make my mind up about. What I love about kids is their naïvety and innocence.

I was walking through the Essex woods with my daughter Alex and my three grandkids when Felix, who was about five years old at the time, asked me to play ninjas with him. I was given a very small twig and asked to sword fight against him holding a rather large branch. Accordingly, he struck me across my knee, and Alex scolded him, saying, "Don't do that to Grandad. He is an old man."

Felix looked up at me with a puzzled look on his face. "How old are you? Ten?"

On a recent visit to see Alex, Lee and the kids, my five year old grand-daughter Cyd stood next to me while I was eating my 'Lillian'. Cyd asked Alex if it was okay to show me something she had learned. Cyd waited until I had finished my dinner and proceeded to spell her name in sign language. I was deeply moved, as I know my parents would have been. It's great that the schools teach signing to the kids today, especially at an early age.

Alex's oldest boy Oscar has always been exceptionally clever. When he was about two he watched me talking to my Parents half in sign language and part lip reading. Oscar got their attention and without a single sound tried to converse with me with lip reading, knowing full well that this was the way to communicate. Both my Parents had tears in their eyes because of his understanding of the situation and I have never forgotten his astute awareness.

Sometime after becoming a widower, I was staying for a weekend with my son Daniel, his wife Daisy and their five-year-old Poppy. I was sitting alone in the front room when Poppy came in with a plate of toast for me.

My Son and Daughter, Alex and Daniel

"I know you miss Nanny Pat and you are lonely, but if you lived with us I would make you tea and toast every day," she said. What a beautiful, thoughtful young lady!

****

My Son Daniel

My relationship with my only Son, Daniel, has been the same as me and my Dad: unconditional love. It would be very difficult to deny he is mine, as it is even more obvious than Kirk and Michael Douglas. He's a lot lighter, but a chip off the old block in many ways. When he is out of order, it delights Janet, my first wife, to say, "Like father, like son."

My Daughter Alex

Big Ben struck 7.45pm on 14 December 1971, and as I looked out of the window of St Thomas's Hospital, old Father Thames seemed to light up as the nurse informed me that I had a baby daughter, my first born. My Alex (only Alexandra when she was naughty) was the most beautiful baby I had ever seen, being obviously biased but why not? She had mauve eyes and a cherub appearance. Even today - still biased - she is not only beautiful, but has the most wonderful nature, which endears her to all and sundry and has never caused me one ounce of trouble. She is a daughter to be proud of!

CHAPTER TWO
The Swinging Sixties

In the pubs and clubs of inner London the talk in the sixties was of the Twins, the Richardsons, the train robbers, and invariably one of the above would walk in with pals. Big talk in the sixties also included, of course, the 1966 World Cup at Wembley, made even better because it was the Germans that we beat. It wouldn't have been the same if the other finalist was either 'Bubble and Squeaks' or the 'Harris Tweeds'. London in the sixties was THE place to be. Everyone was jumping. The ladies, thanks to Mary Quant, were mini-skirted up to the nines and tights had not yet been invented. Stockings still ruled. Thank God.

My fiancée had had enough of me. The way I looked at it, we were both strong-willed individuals and both of us had to have our own way. Marian might have had another view. She was quoted several years later at a reunion of the Peckham Co-op Mods saying that, "she loved me but I was a bastard." In any event, at the age of twenty two, after breaking up with my fiancée, I was a free spirit in London, home of the swinging sixties.

The first thing I did was to upset my lovely Mum twice. I had come home in the early hours from a night out and put the waistcoat of my suit over the back of a chair. I went out at ten on a Sunday morning to play football for my Sunday team on Blackheath. When I came in for my Sunday roast, the Old Man was shaking his head and said in a couple of signs that my Mum wasn't happy with me. Mum was cooking lunch and he said for me to look in my waistcoat pocket. In the top pocket was what was termed in the barbers as a packet of three. Only there was only one left in the packet.

There were three ways of looking at it:

1. I was being smart and taking protection;
2. Did they need to open it up and look?
3. Would it have been okay if there were three still untouched?

It took flowers and chocolates for a week to get forgiveness but something far worse was to happen.

It was New Year's Eve. Mum and Dad, Gran and Grandad, and Uncle Percy were going over to Fat Sid's pub in Bethnal Green. They assured me they were going on to a 'Mori' and wouldn't be home. I was in a club in southeast London and met a vivacious redhead. We both had Champagne and we finished up in bed at the flat over the rag and bone shop. About 4am, I hear a cab pull up and Uncle Percy say, "Good night, cabbie. Happy New Year." Then I hear five people coming up the stairs. My Mum poked her head around the door to wish me a Happy New Year. The redhead froze. My Mum, seeing two heads in the bed, turned the light on. My Mum and Gran are in the forefront of the investigation, and the three men behind them. The three men are smiling, and giving me the thumbs up. My Mum and Gran are raving with me, but feeling a bit sorry for my new friend.

My Mum told me to take the lady home, but I had had a good drink and New Year's cabs were like gold dust. What happened next had to be so embarrassing for the lady: she slept between my Mum and Gran in the double bed. I got up early and took her home in my car. For some reason, she declined to give me her phone number!! I went home and took Gran, Grandad, and Uncle Percy home. The Old

Man smiled. My Mum scowled. It wasn't the best start to a New Year.

Fashion

I was completely absorbed in Mod culture. In London at the time, there wasn't anything you couldn't get made, and made by craftsmen in east end shops at a cut price before being sent up west for the toff shops. As a lifelong follower of styles and fashions, for me the biggest disappointment was the advent of hippies and flower power in the mid-sixties. That whole sartorial scene was a big turn-off: kaftans, flowers in your hair, peace brother V-sign, beads and shoulder length hair.

What it did for me, and many others, was to push us toward the Hollywood look, á la Sinatra and Cary Grant: smart mohair hand-made suits, tab and pin-through collared shirts, top pocket-handkerchiefs, black silk socks, and well-polished shoes, beautifully topped off by the obligatory Burberry coat.

Back in those days, up an alleyway off Prescott Street E1, there was a Burberry warehouse where the goods for the flagship in the Haymarket were made. The only difference between East and West End was the price. Whether this was an illegal operation I'm not too sure! I could have a cashmere classic, fly front, raglan shoulder, Prussian collar overcoat handmade for a 'pony' (£25), which sold up in the West End for a 'tonne' (£100).

What I remember most was the wonderful petite lady who measured and fitted you, and, as she took your 'Nelsons', she always said in a Yiddish accent, "I vish you vell to vear it." I can still see her today in my mind. She was less than five feet tall, very thin, heavily permed hair, sporting a pair of 'cat's eyes' bottle top spectacles that went up in points. A classic East End character with all the hand movements and a great line in chat. She was probably in her mid-sixties, married with kids and grandkids, always asking all the young bucks, "Are you still single? I vould be available if you vanted!" All I could think of was that she was a similar age to my grandmothers, and I always replied, "Let's give it a spin you little minx. Meet me under the clock at Waterloo Station, seven O'clock Monday night." She laughed.

What a sales person! All the boys treated her like royalty. Even today, some fifty years later, we still remember her reminiscing over a drink.

When I wore my new overcoat on a sunny day, I used the adage, "It's always cold when you've got a new overcoat, but it's never cold when you've got a new suit."

For better or worse, I have not wavered in my sartorial preferences some fifty years later, which prompted the comment from my first wife Janet that I am in a time warp, "he dresses early Mafia!" There was never any doubt that I would never walk into a 'tasty' pub in the Old Kent Road or through the turnstiles at Millwall with a flower in my hair!

Better Dead Than Ted!

I always had a thing about clothes, and in 1959 a whole new era was happening. After the Teds, with their velvet-collared drape jackets, brothel creepers, drainpipe trousers and bootlace ties, came the Mods.

As long as you had money in your 'sky', the world, as far as clothing was concerned, was your oyster. There were shirt makers, tailors, cobblers, hatters and milliners, all available at reasonable prices and within the confines of working class areas.

There were hundreds of boys and girls who invented their own styles to show off at the dance halls. The place to be seen in south-east London was the Peckham Co-op, a large dance hall above the Co-op store at the northern end of Rye Lane. It attracted hundreds of teenagers. When you climbed the stairs and paid half a crown (two shillings sixpence) to the heavies seated at a table, a whole new magical world appeared. This was before Carnaby Street. This was the original birthplace of the south-east Mods long before they were depicted in the 1979 film 'Quadraphenia'. These kids were the originals and the film captured the scenes at Brighton beaches between the Rockers and the Mods in 1964.

Other in-places were the Lyceum and the Locarno. They were also places to be seen showing off your latest design from the tailors, who sometimes scoffed when you ordered but after all, money was money to them.

The Peckham Co-op was my favourite haunt. There was a stage with a small band playing the hits of the day and the peacocks strutted their stuff. Some just stood and posed. The aim was to look cool.

At the time, £25 was a popular price for handmade suits, shoes and overcoats. Shirts could be made for less than £2, depending on the material.

The ladies usually made their own clothing, a skill taught to them by their older sisters or mums, or they found seamstresses to make clothes for them.

The boys all had college boy hairstyles á lá Perry Como and wore suits with curved jackets, covered buttons and a half belt at the back. The trousers were straight-legged and had two-inch splits at the bottom, topped off with a covered button. The St Louis' were winkle pickers made in a shop in Battersea called Stan's - the longer the point, the more fashionable the shoe.

All the jackets were just below waist high, supposedly to copy the short Italian style, which was a bit longer. My best pal, Terry 'Tex' Wiltshire outdid everybody by having a suit made with the jacket navel high which he was able to carry off with his slim torso.

These were heady days. Few people used drugs; the closest thing was purple hearts. People enjoyed their times content with a light ale or a spirit.

At the time, I seemed to have a habit of getting thrown down flights of stairs from clubs. The Top Twenty Club in Peckham was a gathering place above shops. One evening there was a live band with a singer called Tommy Bruce, who had a gravelly voice and who had a hit with 'Ain't Misbehavin'. Amongst our eight-strong group of guys there was a pal called Buster Osbourne who thought it funny to drop a stink bomb. I didn't find it too funny and one or two were pointing at me saying, "Look at his face". Out of nowhere came the bouncer, who worked for two famous south-east London brothers, and with a Luger in my back threw me down about fifteen stairs. Being innocent of all charges, I ran back up the stairs, only to see a gun pointing at me. This caused me to do an about-turn. I found out later that this particular bouncer wound up imprisoned on a murder charge in South Africa.

The second flight of stairs I encountered was in a discotheque in Wardour Street, Soho. Terry 'Tex' Wiltshire, my oldest pal since my school days, suggested we go to one of the first discos in London. When you paid to get in, the doorman placed a rubber stamp in the shape of a 'D' on your wrist. We were not well-heeled, so Tex suggested we get a burned out match and mark our wrist with a 'D' in order to 'jib-in'. Up the steep stairs Tex went, and was confronted by Bert Assaratti, the bouncer and one time top wrestler. Somehow, Tex made it in and looked out the window, calling me up. So up I went, completely confident and totally unaware that the stamped 'D' was luminous. I only said, "Alright Bert" before he took my wrist and held it under a light. It was lights out for me lying in a heap at the bottom of the 'apples'.

I had known Tex Wiltshire since we first met at the age of ten at our school outfitters, Pynes in Lewisham Way SE4. We were both in with our mums buying the school uniform. He asked, "Are you going to Addey's?" When I confirmed, he said, "Good, we can be friends." It was a friendship that lasted another forty-seven years until his untimely passing. He was a great personality, a joker and a very good footballer. Anybody who played football in south-east London knew him or of him. He played for non-league teams and only the best Sunday teams. He was a Denis Law lookalike with silky skills to match.

Tex got his nickname, so legend has it, from the New X Texas Rangers, a speedway team next to the home of Millwall F.C. and he was the mascot as a cute small blonde headed boy.

We grew up together and it wasn't possible to dislike anything about him. He was full of cheek as a youngster and got away with it because of his personality. To give you some idea of his cheek and sense of humour, one lunch time in the early sixties, before mobiles were invented, we were on our way to the Lyceum. I was on the back of his scooter outside the Law Courts at the top of Fleet Street. Alongside us came a chauffeur-driven Rolls Royce with a very solemn looking man in the back seat. He looked as if he could have been a judge at the Big House. Quick as a flash, Tex pulled out a telephone with a loose cord from a box at the front of his Lambretta. He tapped on the window of the passenger and holding up the phone he said, "It's for you." Judge Rolls wound the window down and put his hand out to take the phone.

We didn't stop laughing until we got to the Ly.

He married Christine who was the love of his life and I was his best man. They had three children and I was delighted that they called their only son Lewis, after me.

Just before he passed at the age of fifty seven, unaware of what was around the corner, he said, "I don't drink or smoke, I'm so healthy I will die of nothing." He did well in life and had a beautiful home with a swimming pool, a great example of a man coming from a poor part of London and doing well for his wife and family, on whom he doted.

Never was the saying 'he could sell ice to the Eskimos' so true. Tex was a great salesman. We all miss him today sixteen years on.

All over inner London there were trendy pubs, mostly owned by 'faces' from the world of sport or the underworld. These pubs had small, wall jukeboxes playing the top tunes, and as the night went on, people sang along to Tony Bennett's 'San Francisco' and other hit numbers. The punters were all part of a fashion parade and usually big spenders. At closing time, 11pm back then, we all looked for 'afters', where the guvnor locked the door and carried on serving. There were groups of drinkers and we had a whip-round for the kitty, which was kept in a pint mug and this kept the guvnor happy knowing he was getting his end.

At the time I drank vodka and lemonade with plenty of 'Vincent' and a slice of lemon. I liked to use the same goblet-style glass all night. The publican obliged and topped up my glass with the mix, and always another slice of lemon. At going home time, I counted the slices of lemon and knew just how many drinks I had had at that session - just a silly idiosyncrasy that amused me.

The ladies were all very fashionable and wore good 'Tom'. I woke up one morning and at the side of my bed with my money and watch was a gold bracelet with about ten gold sovereigns on it. I went into the kitchen and put the bracelet in my Mum's hand, saying it was a present for her. She knew I was joking and insisted I take it back to its rightful owner, which I did that evening.

The lady in question and I were in a cab in a clinch in the backseat when the bracelet caught the side of my face, so she took it off. I walked her to the door and asked the cab to wait. When I was on the way home, I spied the bracelet in the corner of the seat. At 3am I didn't fancy waking her dad who was a market porter and a bull of a man.

Lesley

One Saturday evening, I was out in Manchester with Big Peter Warden, a good friend and London cab driver, and two ladies we had met in Majorca earlier in the year. We were in the top club, back then called The Phonograph, which was frequented by the local celebs, such as, on the night, George Best, Mike Summerbee and the DJ Pete Murray. My lady, Lesley, a lovely redhead who did some modelling, introduced us to George. Amongst his entourage were two guys with flowers in their hair – very trendy, but I doubt if they would have made it through the night down the Kings Arms on the Old Kent Road.

In the 1942 film, 'Casablanca', Conrad Veidt, playing the Nazi German Major Strasser, mockingly says to Bogart, "Could you see us in New York?" To which Bogart replies with the lines of, "There are parts of New York I wouldn't advise you to invade," probably thinking of the Bronx or Brooklyn. So, to those who cast aspersions on so-called 'soft southerners', I say in my best Bogart lisp, "Try Bermondsey and Bethnal Green. They will give you a warm welcome."

Lesley and I saw each other for a few months. She spent her twenty first birthday with me and her parents at the 'Talk of the Town' in London. I flew up for long weekends, staying at the Midland Hotel, but in the end it went the way of most holiday romances. It was inevitable that the distance between us would make it impossible. Plus, if I missed the last bus, the cab fare would be a bit 'Anna May'.

At the time, I was living over the rag and bone shop in SE4 and in the market. Lesley's parents were very much up-market, living in the stockbroker belt in Cheshire.

Her mother was lovely and we got on well. Her father was a successful businessman on the board of a motor manufacturer, and wanted someone better for his only child which was quite understandable. So, being a jump in front of him, I covered the angles on the night of Lesley's twenty first: I knew he would make himself busy and would insist on dropping me off in the cab, just to see where I lived, before going to his Mayfair hotel. My very good pal and best man at my first wedding, Jimmy Scullion, lived in Albany Street, Regents Park in the council flats, on the opposite side of which was Millionaire's Row, with mansions facing the park. I had made arrangements to stay with Jim and he left the key under the street doormat. I kissed Lesley and her ma goodnight and shook hands with daddy, who was surveying the area. I walked towards Millionaire's Row with a confident swagger and out of sight into a mews. I gave it five minutes, making sure the cab had gone, then crossed the road into the council estate and a good night's kip.

Some years later I laughed, as it was déjà vu for Rodney in 'Only Fools and Horses'. Rodney wanted to impress a lady but didn't have my 'donald duck' and got caught in the teeming rain.

Brighton Fairies

On another occasion, I was in Brighton for a weekend with my fiancée Marian, and we were looking for a night's accommodation. Marian was a hairdresser, a very stylish dresser and was very handy at making her own clothes. When I picked her up for a night out, I never knew what colour her 'barnet' would be: it could be blonde, pink, lilac. You couldn't second guess it. On the night in question, she had on a gold sparkling shirt waister dress and her hair was a blonde beehive with side flick ups. She looked the business. Walking around the back streets just off the front, I spied a sign that said 'Vacancies'. We knocked on the door and stood back. An eight year old girl opened the door and I asked if her mum was in. She stood there open-mouthed looking Marian up and down, and shouted, "mum, there's a fairy at the door." I know she isn't talking about me but it leads on nicely.

The landlady came to the door and said there was a room upstairs for Marian and I could share the front room with another fellow. After inspecting the room and agreeing terms, I was shown into my lodgings for the night.

My room-mate for the night was a Brummie, and as Brighton was the gay capital of England, it didn't exactly surprise me that he was 'Doris Day'. Donnie explained that he was down to visit his boyfriend and he asked if I wanted the sofa or the camp bed. Appropriately, he took the latter.

The next day, whilst promenading along the front, I heard, "yoo hoo!" Never one to be homophobic, Marian and I took them for a drink and amongst the "I love your hair" (not to me) and the "I love your shoes" (yes, to me), we had a great afternoon. The boys were great company at a time when things in the sixties were not so open as they are today.

I have to confess that once when I was in Hong Kong on business I pretended to be gay under extenuating circumstances. I was in the bar of a good hotel when I was approached by a 'China Doll' who asked if I was interested in any business. After declining her offer I had a couple more ladies standing next to me with the same proposition. I was going out for dinner and as my exit line I said, "Sorry to waste your time, ladies, but I am gay."

One of them said, "I send my brother round." Was that determination to get some business or to keep it in the family?

Poor Diction

I was collecting a girlfriend for a night out, but I had only taken her home once before. I knocked at the house I thought she lived in and a small red-headed man answered the door.

"Hello, the name of O'Neill?" I said, thinking it could be her father. He shook his head and closed the door in my face. After finding the right house, which was next door, I was in the front room being introduced to mum and dad, when there was a knock at the street door. The young lady's dad was having a conversation in the hall when the door opened and in came the little man with ginger hair. "That's him," he said, pointing at me. He told the young lady's father, "Be careful. There's a suspicious looking character asking for Herne Hill."

Caravans

In the sixties every man and his dog seemed to own a caravan, so renting one for a week or a weekend was easy. The caravans were not as they are today, with a couple of bedrooms, showers and toilets all in house. Back then, all campers shared communal toilets and wash basins, all very basic.

So one Friday night we arrived at Leysdown, Little Jim, me and two young ladies. Jim snaffled the only bed and I had the long covered board that passed for a settee in the main area. In the middle of the night, the young lady sharing my board asked her if I would give her a piggyback over to the ladies' toilets. Being a gentleman, I put on my new Chelsea boots and waded into the mud with my lady astride my back. It was about 3am and as we opened the door to the van, we could hear heavy breathing coming from the executive bedroom. I thought to myself "good luck, Jimmy". The next morning, while the ladies were in the washroom, I said to Jimmy, "You cracked it last night, all that heavy breathing." He looked despondent and replied, "Turn it in, I should be so lucky. She's got asthma."

The Krays

Since my teens, I had been in the same environment as the Twins, but not as 'Chinas', more as on onlooker at their antics. In the early to mid-sixties, it was not easy to avoid their presence. Any popular pub or club where we all wanted to be were also their favourite haunts and none more so than the Grave Maurice pub in Whitechapel.

I remember vividly that the pub had one long bar and the guvnor was a convivial man called Alan. He told me a story that one day Ronnie wanted to send a telegram to Sophie Tucker, the great music hall artiste, who was appearing at the London Palladium. Ronnie wrote out his text and spelt the singer's name as 'Soapy'. Alan took the text and phoned the telegram over, with Ronnie leaning over the bar to make sure the telegram was sent. The telephonist asked Alan to spell the name out, and, with Ronnie is still breathing down Alan's neck, the telegram went out to 'Soapy Tucker'.

It was a small pub, but at the time very trendy. There were a few booths along the bar and two toilets at the end. The door from the street would open on a regular basis by a minder who would proceed to walk the length of the bar, go into both toilets, before commandeering a booth, having first ensured there were no enemies of his charges afoot. After a couple of minutes, in would walk the Twins attired in full regalia. Sadly, for Alan, his other customers would slowly drift out of the pub, without making it too obvious.

Numerous books have been written about the Krays, and all and sundry know the fear they induced. My two favourite stories about the Twins had fear in them, but which served to do some good.

TALES FROM THE RANKS AND BEYOND | 129

Tex Wiltshire, Peckham Co-op Mods and his scooter

Micky Murray, Peckham Co-op Mods and his scooter

On holiday with John Berry and Jimmy Thomas (pictures above and below) at a holiday camp in 1960

Tex and Marian, circa 1961

At a 'Moriarty' with Ollie Smith, Peter Warden and Jock Scullion

Mayfair night club with pals and Janet, my first wife (centre)

An elderly lady who lived in the neighbourhood had been burgled and went to see Violet Kray, a kind woman who was the Twin's mother. Violet called Ronnie to the parlour to hear her story.

"I lost £100 in savings and my television set, which was black and white."

Ronnie opened the parlour window and whispered to members of the Firm who were standing outside on the pavement, "Go and find out who did it."

A few days go by and a young man was brought to Fort Vallance, as the Twin's residence was called. After some 'treatment', the man was told to come back with £200 and a colour television set.

"But it was only £100 and the set was an old black and white," the thief complained.

To which Ronnie replied, "You're not listening, son. You've got a week to put right your damage. You don't steal from our manor or off your own people. Go over to Kensington or Knightsbridge, where they are insured and can afford it." The final word was one week or no kneecaps. Within days, the thief had made full repayment.

The second story was that one of the Forty Thieves gang, a top shoplifter who supplied Violet, came in with two black eyes. Ronnie was called in and asked her what was the story. The story was that she lived with a violent man who beat her up after his drinking sessions.

Ronnie said, "You can't go to Harrods or Harvey Nichols with shiners. I'll sort it."

The lady 'hoister' asked him not to, but it fell on deaf ears. The next Sunday morning, the Twins knocked on the door and, in their usual manner, warned the woman's partner to lay off. Weeks went by and the woman was drinking tea with Mrs Kray after concluding business. Ronnie came in and asked if all was well.

She said, "Well, after you paid him a visit, he came home drunk from the pub and gave me terrible verbal abuse, but no violence. I took this to mean he hadn't learnt his lesson, so I hit him over the head with a vase for good measure." Shortly afterwards, their relationship was over, but he never lifted his hands to her again.

In all people there is some good. It's just that we have to look a bit deeper at times.

CHAPTER THREE
Stories, Characters and Likeable Rogues

Trigger's Double

This cab driver came into the cafe and was always worth a good laugh, but you had to contain the laughter. He would pontificate and say, "My family were big in France years ago. They had a big gateaux near Calais." Another gem was the boys all went to Spain for a golfing week and involved with the club was the famous golfer, Henry Cotton. Trigger Mark II said to Henry, "I love your radio show on Sunday mornings" finishing up with an impersonation of Billy Cotton 'wakey wakey'.

Big Ted

A tall lean Jason Statham lookalike and a man of few words, Big Ted was driving his cab in Wandsworth, when a Jack the Lad in a Roller with a blonde in tow cut him up. There were angry words and the JTL pointed to where he wanted Ted to pull over. Ted got out of his cab and leant against a wall with his arms folded. The JTL ran up to him, very animated, and with a few choice words, aimed a blow at Ted. Ted only hit him once but it was enough. When the JTL came round, the blonde had his head in her lap and he looked up at Ted.

"You were a bit hasty," he said.

"I wasn't holding any interviews."

Party Time

In the early sixties, I was at a party in Camberwell Green, south-east London, with my fiancé who was beautiful, and a bit on the 'Gunga Din' side. We were dancing and a voice over my shoulder said, "Who's he dancing with? Olive Oyl?" My lady was most indignant and expected me to start a battle, until I turned around and said to the voice, "Oh, hallo Charlie." End of party – goodnight!

It was Charlie Richardson, who, along with his brother Eddie, ran south-east London.

The Tie

One Saturday night we were drinking in the Kings Arms pub in the Old Kent Road. At closing time we were all outside on the pavement when I was approached by a couple of good friends, who were well known to me and to the local constabulary. They were off up West to a night club but weren't wearing ties, so they asked to borrow my tie and the tie of my pal, Little Jimmy.

Now, I had bought my tie in Burlington Arcade, Piccadilly, and I loved it: a beautiful knitted mauve silk with white polka dots, which cost me £15 (in 1962), it was the best tie I've ever had.

Something happened to my two pals, and they weren't seen again for some eight years (read between the lines!). Ten years later, I was driving my cab in King William Street, City of London, and at the right-hand side of me was a Bentley. On closer examination, I saw it was the deadly duo. I banged on the window, they put the window down and said, "Look who it is!"

I said, "Don't mind all that. Where's my fucking tie?"

Lots of laughter as they drove away.

The Guest House

There was a good friend of mine, who was a docker and who became a successful publican in the East End. He was a hard man and an acquaintance of Ronnie Kray. Years went by and I didn't see him for some time. One day I spied him in Bond Street in a convertible, a Yankee job, with a male passenger. Unable to speak because I had a fare in the back, we acknowledged each other.

Later, I picked up a mutual friend in my cab, who said, "Did you hear about Johnnie H? He has come out, now lives in Brighton with his partner and runs a guest house." Being curious and unable to believe the transition, I enquired what the name of the guesthouse was - 'Fred and Breakfast'.

As a postscript, the fellow now lives in Spain happily with his partner, and the mutual friend who told me is a legend in the East End. He had the biggest Roman nose ever seen and had a nose job. Rumour has it he went to the mid-Atlantic and had it blasted.

The Wrong Man

My wife Pat had a friend who was a school teacher and taught in the Gorbals in Glasgow. She also told many a good tale, which captured the times and the area. She was telling a class of six year olds the story of the three little pigs, and in the front row a little boy with a runny nose sat cross-legged, deeply engrossed with the fairy tale. She had the impression that this little boy had never heard anything like this before. When she got to the part of the story where "he huffed and he puffed and he blew the house down", the little fellow, genuinely moved, said, "the rotten bastard."

This same lady, who was very dignified and a good churchgoer, was at the swimming baths with her husband and two young daughters, larking about, splashing and ducking. She suddenly dived under the water, swam towards her husband, and pulled his swimming trunks down. Emerging from the water, she saw her husband sitting at the side of the pool yards away! Red face!

Mistaken Identity

Patsy McCarthy and I were in the Blind Beggar pub in Whitechapel on a Saturday night. I was wearing a Burberry trench mac and Patsy a cashmere overcoat. The door opened and in came a face that worked in Covent Garden market, one that I recognised and knew well. To say that the face had a reputation and was a psycho would be an understatement.

The pub was heaving. It was one big bar full of trendy people done up to the nines, drinking shoulder to shoulder. The face came through the crowd and stopped a few feet away from me. He drew a cutlass from the side of his trousers and slashed his victim across the chest twice. Girls screamed and ran into the toilets. Blood splashed everywhere, especially on me and Patsy: both overcoats were ruined. The victim was taken to hospital, the bar staff cleaned up and normal services resumed.

On Monday morning at 3am, I was on my stand in Covent Garden market when along came the face who doubtless had seen me in the pub on Saturday night.

"Were you out on Saturday, Rog?"

"Not me – I was in watching Match of the Day."

"Thank you. Bye."

Clearly a case of mistaken identity on my part!

Monpeys Umple

There was a young fella who played in the same football team as me and his uncle was my good pal. Unfortunately, the young man had a slight speech impediment and was always struggling to get his words out right. His favourite expression was "Well, I'll be a monpey's umple." He worked for a big bank as a messenger and was married but struggled to make ends meet. So, out of desperation he put a stocking on his face to disguise his features, went to the counter at the bank where he worked, and demanded the cash from the till. The teller, recognising his voice, didn't even look up and said, "Freddie, behave yourself and stop larking about. Can't you see I'm busy." Fred slunk away, happy that everybody concerned treated it as a joke and he wasn't facing porridge.

The Boxing Promoter

Once a year, normally in January when the cab trade was quiet, we would have our 'office Christmas party' in Michael Caine's restaurant, Langan's, in Mayfair. There would be ten to twelve cab drivers, all suited and booted, and the boat would be well and truly pushed out. For three years on the trot, we would be drinking at the bar and the famous boxing promoter, Mickey Duff, would approach us to get in the company.

He was a nice man and good company, relating boxing stories and old East End characters that he knew. He was also a lonely man, and asked if he could join us for dinner. I sat next to him and over the course of three hours and a lot of booze and storytelling, he would say at intervals, "Rog,

I met a lady who is seventy years old, but looks fifty." An hour passed and he said, "Rog, I met a lady who is seventy but only looks forty." Half an hour passed, more booze, and he said, "Rog, I met a lady who is seventy but only looks thirty." Another thirty minutes and he said, "Rog, I met a lady who is seventy but only looks...."

"Stop right there, mate," I said. "I don't want you up on a charge with a minor!"

The Man who Shot Liberty Valance

Grandad Rogers lived all his life never allowing anyone to 'take a liberty'. This perspective was instilled in me at an early age, as with Jimmy Ennis, "Out you go, he's took a liberty with you and bosh him." So, having been brain washed, I would often quote 'he's took a liberty' in the company of my pals and would have to live up to the bravado.

There was a family of four brothers from Deptford, a tough manor. The three older ones were useful with their fists and looked after their kid brother, a twenty year old and Jack the Lad who played on the fact that he had heavy protection.

I was eighteen and was in a club with my future fiancée, who the JTL was very attracted to. He said to my lady,

"What do you see in a silly little boy like that?" I smiled and choked back my rage. He'd 'took a liberty'. To this day, only one pal, the lady and I know the story of what happened next. It was a bit 'iffy' to brag about.

My Dad's pal, Frank, brought a stocking round to the house one night to show what robbers wore. We all had a good laugh at how we all couldn't be identified, looking grotesque the tighter we pulled it over the face.

I knew where this particular JTL lived and bided my time.

It was a Friday night and he was a bit tipsy. A figure appeared out of nowhere with a stocking on its face. It only took one strike on his hooter and he went down.

Several weeks passed and I was in a club when the JTL came in. After a while he acknowledged me.

I said, "Hello, mate, how are you? You look a bit different."

"Yes, I got attacked and robbed one night."

"Robbed!"

"And got me hooter done."

"Who done you?"

"I don't know."

"Well, if I hear anything I'll let you know."

"Thanks, mate."

His nose was broken and apparently his ego has taken a knock as well. My lady openly wasn't pleased but deep down I think she was.

Revenge is a dish best served cold, so they say.

Spivs

A younger cab driver once asked me what a 'spiv' was. The best way to describe a spiv would be to see the character George Cole played in 'St Trinians': a trilby hat, a thin pencilled moustache on the top lip, á la Errol Flynn, and a well-padded double breasted overcoat.

These guys worked out of suitcases on the corners of busy shopping centres, like Oxford Street, and sold things that were rationed or difficult to get. Silk stockings for the ladies were very popular with a never-ending demand before and after World War II. The spivs had no overheads – their wares were stolen goods - had a look-out for the police and could close the suitcase and 'have it away on their toes' at the drop of a hat. Their number grew in leaps and bounds, so much so that it was strongly rumoured that the police set up a special branch to just to deal with them, called 'Suspicious Persons Itinerate Vending'; and it was said that's how their name came about.

When I was seventeen, I had shirts made out of a suitcase by two working on the corner of Old Castle Street in Petticoat Lane. You ordered your shirt material on Sunday morning; one measured your neck and chest, whilst the other looked out for the police among the bustle of Petticoat Lane. The following Sunday, without fail, they would be there with your shirt for one pound and ten shillings. They obviously had access to a shirt maker, and they made a living.

At the time, 1959, Perry Como was a big crooner, and the Mods copied his hairstyle, casual cardigans and shirts with initials. I would get a casual, long collared shirt from the two spivs, and a cardigan, a look that today would be described as 'smart casual'. When I took the goods home, my Mum would sew on my initials.

With my interest in fashion, there was always some icon's haircut that we tried to copy: the Teds had the 'Tony Curtis' and the Mods the 'Perry Como'. Nowadays, I ask my son,

"Who is responsible for the style of short back and sides, and the number ones?" It's probably someone who is losing or lost his 'barnet', like Bruce Willis.

Irish jigs are definitely a no-no. One of the worst was surely Francis Albert's, and him with all his millions!

The Sting

The best story about forged notes came from a good friend of mine, who is sadly no longer with us. My old pal was going on holiday to America for ten days and had acquired twenty snide $50 greenbacks. He explained that, at the time, detection wasn't as sophisticated as it is today.

He finished his holiday with a three day cruise in the Caribbean and was drinking in the bar with a New York policeman and the two wives. The fifty-dollar 'Jekyll and Hydes' were going over the bar like wildfire with the change making everything kosher. About an hour from the first call for docking, there was an announcement over the ship's tannoy, "There will be a delay in disembarking when we arrive at Fort Lauderdale."

My pal panicked and thought that the barman had sussed the fake bills. He went to toilet and put the remaining notes down the pan. He went back to the bar and another announcement came over the tannoy, "There will be a delay in disembarking at Fort Lauderdale as the cases were loaded the wrong way."

Is Glaswegian a Foreign Language

After the sickness scheme was, established for a couple of years, the LTDA began to get overtures from other cab trade bodies. Glasgow, Edinburgh and Dublin all made contact with us, interested in having benefits for their membership.

I had never been to Scotland before. Bill Thorpe (later on page 319) and I attended a meeting called by the White Flag Cab Association at their headquarters in the Gorbals area of Glasgow. There were us two sitting at one end of a boardroom table and eight Glaswegians around the rest of the table. Everyone was suited and booted.

The meeting was chaired by Alan Gracie, an ex-Glaswegian police officer. Alan opened the meeting in a broad Glaswegian accent, which for us two, was not understandable. Out of the corner of my mouth, I whispered to Bill, "What the fuck did he say?"

"I don't know," replied Bill, equally perplexed.

Unfortunately, our stage whispers were heard around the table, and laughter erupted. We never looked back: it was a constructive meeting with plenty of translations from both sides. These guys were top men, and thirty years later I still have contact with those who are still living.

One of the members of the White Flag committee was a gentleman called George, who, in a previous occupation worked on cruise ships as a singer and impressionist. Having seen him in action, I can tell you he was good. Unfortunately, George had a terrible stutter when he spoke, but not when he sang.

So, on his first day at a committee meeting, Alan Gracie welcomed him, saying, "George, welcome, and please if you wish to contribute to the debate, for fuck's sake sing it!"

One night I was taken to a Glaswegian singing pub where singers were called up from the floor to sing on stage. For me, a stranger in a tough part of Glasgow, I needed to stay sober and behave myself.

A couple of tables in front of me sat a couple in their thirties. She was a nice-looking girl but he was a bit out of date, being an Elvis lookalike, and they were having a 'bull and cow'. The MC called him up to sing and she came over to our table and asked me to dance. Weighing up the situation, I declined.

My four Glaswegian cab driving pals were smiling and one said, "You can't knock her back. You have to get up." So I did. Fred Astaire never had any competition from me: I only did close dancing.

Elvis was crooning, "Are you lonesome tonight" and giving me daggers. The more daggers he threw, the tighter she clung to me. At the end of his crooning, I walked her back to her table and returned to my pals. The lovebirds made up and were on the floor dancing to a slow one. As she passed our table, she gave me a wink. Did I feel used?

The Crying Game
Dublin notables: James Joyce, George Bernard Shaw, WB Yeats, Oscar Wilde & the IRA.

Glaswegian boys are all larger than life.

So too are Dublin committee men. I was invited to their headquarters to discuss the sickness scheme and was met at the airport by my minder for the next two days. He was a big man, who had been an Army boxing champion. During the journey into the city form the airport, I asked him why I needed a minder. That night it became apparent.

After the meeting, I was driven to my hotel to shower and change before we went to eat. The minder waited outside. After a good meal, we went to a pub with karaoke. Two of the Dublin committee men got up at intervals with the same introduction by the MC, "And here he is, the singing taxi man!" Both of them sang the old Tammy Wynette standard 'Stand by Your Man', which I thought was a strange choice for two muscular tough guys.

When the pub closed, we went to a club, which I can only describe as a speakeasy in a dodgy manor of Dublin. When Tim O' Leary knocked on the door, a sliding flap was opened and a face behind it peered out. Recognising Timmo, the face said, "Timmo, come on in." The first thing I saw was an old man sleeping on the floor with his head resting on a cushion. The club was similar to some of the 'drinkers' I had been in years before in London.

We were all having a great time drinking vodka and red. Everybody took turns in giving a song without any musical accompaniment. When I sang an old Cockney song, two things happened. The old boy on the floor woke up and came over to speak to me, telling me he had lived at the Elephant and Castle and had seen Millwall play. I bought him a drink.

Out of nowhere a pugnacious looking 'ice cream' came over and said, "You've just took the Falklands. I suppose you want Ireland as well."

"Not at all, mate. Have a drink?" I replied.

"The IRA will know about you," he said and left the club.

Twenty minutes later the door came open and in came my new acquaintance. I'm thinking "he's probably got a shooter." My minder headed towards him and they spoke. The minder let him come towards me and he said, "I'm out of order. Let me buy you a drink." We shook hands and all was water under the bridge, but I have to admit, at one stage I thought I was going to have to change my trousers.

Dino

When I was a kid we watched Dean Martin and Jerry Lewis at the Saturday morning pictures. I loved Jerry and thought Dean was just a stooge in the same way Abbott was for Costello or Little Ernie was for Eric. In later life, it was a complete reversal.

The three singers that I idolised when I was in my twenties were Francis Albert, Tony Bennett and Dino. I always put Sinatra at the top of my list until one night in Vegas.

I was representing the LTDA at a worldwide convention for the cab trade in Las Vegas. The Aussies, the Canadians, French, Italians, Germans and Americans from all the major cities were in attendance. The Yanks hosted the conference and really pushed the boat out in true Vegas style. The conference was a useful get-together, and business concepts for the taxi trade were discussed with the use of interpreters.

When I got up to speak, I delivered my best line and got no response for a couple of minutes, which threw me until the non-English speakers received a translation.

After the meeting, a Chicago gentleman who had, what looked like a dead cat on his head, approached me and asked me to join him for a drink in the bar. He informed me he was the biggest cab advertiser in the States and wanted to get advertising on the cabs in London. The drawback to his request was that his advertising took the shape of a triangle that sat on the roof of the cab. He asked me to see if this was feasible for the London cab. I said I would look into it, knowing full well it didn't stand a chance with the Public Carriage Office in London at that time. This guy with the 'Irish Jig' on his head was desperate and saw the million dollar signs coming up.

We arranged to meet, and he took me to see Dino at the old MGM Grand Hotel. There was a queue of people going right out of the door, but in 'Good Fella' style we walked right past and to the front. He deposited several green bills into the hand of the maître d'. A table was placed in the front of the diners, almost at the stage.

The next sixty minutes were just magic.

The MC said, "Ladies and Gentlemen, the star of our show, direct from the bar – Dean Martin!"

Out came the King of Cool, with drink and cigarette, acting the drunk. His first words were to the band, "How long I been on, pallie?"

He sang, drank, smoked and took the pee out of his pal, Francis Albert. It was a memorable performance that outshone a Sammy Davis evening I had seen in London in the sixties.

After that night, I relegated Sinatra to my number two singer, a decision that still causes heavy debate with my brother in law, Jim McCully, and my good pal, Brian Owen. Brian being an Arsenal man and a football scout, reckons that my team, Millwall, are a pub side and Dino is just a pub singer. Sinatra is often copied well, but I have yet to hear a good Dino impersonator. People think Dino copied Bing Crosby but he puts his voice down to the lead singer of the Mills Brothers.

Liverpool F.C. and the Canadian Connection

My old pal Mickey Murray moved to Canada about forty years ago and made a good life for himself in Toronto working for the Arrow Shirt Company. The first time the family visited him my kids were five and seven years old, and we stayed with him and his wife, Diane, at their home on the Beaches.

Mickey was a lifelong Millwall man, and when he came home to visit his parents in Peckham, it coincided with the Liverpool versus Millwall game at Anfield. On the phone we decided to go to the match and Mickey wrote to Anfield for three tickets: one for each of us and one for his pal in Toronto who was a Scouser and was coming home to put a headstone on his mother's grave. In his letter he asked if we could get a tour of the grounds and trophy room before the match. By reply, he received three tickets enclosed in an unfranked white envelope, with no compliment slip or headed Liverpool F.C. paper and postage stamps. At the time, nothing was thought about the shabby reply, although with such a big club as Liverpool, we expected better.

On the Saturday of the game, I was doing a seminar for credit unions in Manchester, which finished at noon. Mickey met me in Manchester and we drove to Merseyside in my car, met his Scouser pal, and the three of us set off for the ground. I had a cashmere overcoat and a Cohiba cigar, and Mickey a full length leather trench coat. As we walked to the ground, little kids about twelve years old greeted us with "Fuck off Cockney bastards". I suppose the attire was the giveaway. We got to our seats in the stands, which were to the left of the famous Kop. In front of our seats were three empty seats that were filled shortly before kick off by five Scousers about forty years old and looking more than a bit useful.

Millwall were bottom of the League and the thousands of diehard Millwall supporters returned the Liverpool chant of "going down, going down" with "so are we, so are we". We got thumped 4–1, and at the end of the game we were tailed by the five Scouse heavies into a tight alleyway leading out of the ground, surrounded by red and white scarves. Suddenly, a cry from one of the famous five went up, "Millwall, Millwall", pointing at us. A scuffle ensued with punches, and I felt a hand in my pocket. We managed to get away without anybody chasing us, and wondering why not. Moving a bit lively, the three of us got to our parked car. I lost no valuables nor did Mickey, but sadly, the Scousers had robbed one of their own of his mum's headstone money.

Putting two and two together, it became clear that Mickey's letter requesting the tickets had been intercepted, and, thinking we were three Canadian tourists, the heavy mob bought three seats in front of us with the aim of securing an easy score.

We drove back to London, thanking our lucky stars we didn't get a serious doing. That was my first visit to Anfield and definitely my last. Give me the safety of the Den anytime!

Sadly, Mickey lost his wife some time ago and has been seeking female company lately. Whenever he phones, we laugh a lot about old faces and times, and I always ask him about his sex life. His usual patter goes, "I met this lady, Phyllis, and have been taking her out."

"What's she look like, Mickey?"

"Great body."

"Yes, Mickey, but what does she look like?"

"Great body." No more information is forthcoming.

Every time I ask him the lady's name, it's always Gladys, Ada, Maude or Daphne, all names belonging to a past generation and I get the mental picture of a sixty year old but nevertheless with a great body.

Stuck in the Smoker With You

When I travelled to and from London visiting my Parents, I always booked a first class smoking seat after an unfortunate experience in second class to be related later. It was at the time when smokers were becoming lepers and the first class section was down to a very few seats. Just as the train was leaving Euston, I was joined by a Him and Her; I would guess by their accents they were from Knightsbridge or Belgravia.

She said, "Oh, dahh..ling, we are in the smoking area."

"It was all I could get," he said.

After breakfast, another couple lit up their smokes, and I went for a light entertainment cigar, nothing Cuban, nothing Churchill, waiting for a comment that wasn't long in coming.

"Oh, I do wish you wouldn't smoke," she said to me.

"Darling, I wish I was six foot four inches tall, but it ain't going to happen."

They left, not to be seen again, and learning not to enforce their upper class will on a poor peasant who took the time and money to get his requirements right for a five and a half hour journey.

First Class Man on a Second Class Train

I was in the second class section of the Euston to Glasgow train, and it was fairly crowded. Opposite me was an elderly lady, leaving two empty seats on our table. On the adjacent table, there was an Asian man, a young lady with a baby and an elderly couple in their late sixties. When we got to Crewe, a small lady with scars on her face sat next to the elderly lady opposite me and a man of about forty sat next to me.

The man's suit was similar to a demob suit, about thirty years old and with a check that no self-respecting man, except for Ted Bovey in 'Hi Dee Hi', would wear. I got the impression he was just out of doing porridge.

Up to our arrival at Crewe Station, everyone was convivial and I was reading a book. As soon as the train pulled out, I sensed it would all change.

The man in the demob suit next to me pulled out a bottle of Whyte and Mackay's whiskey and took three large gulps. I knew it wouldn't be long before he started a conversation with me. He stuck the bottle under my chin and said, "Wanna swallee?" in a broad Glaswegian accent. Very politely I replied, "No thanks mate. I'm driving at the other end."

He did his best Dick Van Dyke Cockney accent.

"No fanks mate."

I smiled but I knew it wasn't going to last. Some time, and a half bottle of whiskey, later, he started, indiscriminately. Everybody was waiting.

"You! Yer fucking Paki bastard," he said to the Asian man, who looked deeper into his 'linen draper'.

"Maggie Thatcher is a c...."

The faces of my fellow travellers were now purple.

I whispered in his ear, "Turn it in mate, there's no need for the language in front of the ladies."

"When we get to Glasgow you're getting a doing."

"I don't think so. I'm off in Motherwell and with all that booze inside of you, you're not capable."

With that, he poked his left index finger in my right eye. My right fist smashed his left eye and I was on top of him in the aisle, using both fists to his face. I could hear a bit of screaming from the ladies and unbeknownst to me the train was pulling into Carlisle Station. The elderly man brought a policeman onto the train and he said, "That's enough, stop it."

The old lady who sat opposite me told the policeman what had happened – swearing, drunken behaviour and how I was attacked in the first instance and not to blame.

The policeman took the drunk off the train and cuffed him. He had left both his shoes on the floor, and, as he was slumped against a column on the platform, I slung the shoes at him to compensate for my red, raw eye.

I sat down again and apologised to my fellow travellers for the disturbance, and they all thanked me, offering cold drinks and food. I said to the little lady with the scarred face, "Why didn't you get off with him at Carlisle?"

"I wasn't with him. He tried to chat me up at Crewe and I sat in the only seat available, do me a favour with a suit like that."

We both laughed.

That was the last time I travelled second class from London to Scotland.

When I got home, the eye was closed and weeping. When I related the full story, it was greeted with uproarious laughter, "He poked you in the eye? He couldn't have been a real Glaswegian or you would've had a Glasgow kiss."

Engaged to Andre Previn

A very nice young lady who was neighbour of ours in Beckenham came up to me, very excited, to tell me she had just gotten engaged to a conductor. Now, she was at the Royal College of Music and her dad was a bank manager. So, keeping a straight face, I said, "Oh, lovely, I am pleased for you. What number bus does he work on?"

Not seeing the leg pull, she said, "Oh no, not on the buses" and did an impersonation of Andre Previn conducting the Royal Philharmonic Orchestra on the pavement.

Doctor in the House

I went to a party one night in a very upmarket area in Chislehurst. I knocked on the door, with my bag of booze for the night and when the door opened, I asked for my host. A very pompous man opened the door and said, "Have you got the right house?" As I was suited and booted, I felt insulted but I bided my time. Later in the evening, I was with a group of men drinking in the kitchen when the 'door man' announced he was a doctor. As quick as a wink I said, "Oh really? What dock's that, my Uncle George works in Millwall docks."

"No, no, I said a doctor."

Looking him up and down with his shabby appearance, I said, "Really? Are you sure? I could have sworn I've seen you in the Red Lion pub next to the Docks Gates."

"No, no, I am definitely a doctor," he cried, almost pleading for me to believe him.

Mission accomplished and an enjoyable party amongst the toffs.

Max Bygraves

I came round Belgrave Square about midday, and there he was in a full length fur coat and a big hat. You couldn't go to a party in our neck of the woods in the fifties and sixties without 'sing along a Max' getting the party dancing and singing along. Max Bygraves was from Bermondsey, a local boy made good, which he wasn't slow in telling me.

"Tin Pan Alley, boy." 'Boy' was a Cockney term of endearment.

"Right-o, Max. How's it going?"

That's all it took for him to tell me, "Course you know, boy, I'm a millionaire. Flat in Belgrave Square, house in Eastbourne. In Australia, I'm bigger than Sinatra. The old blue rinses love me."

For me, I was delighted to meet a local boy who made good. I knew his brother who had the Breakspeare Arms and who was also a good singer, but Max got all the breaks.

With the "Course you know I'm a millionaire" ringing in my ears, I pulled up in Tin Pan Alley.

"How much, Boy?"

"Three shillings, nine pence, Max."

"Take four shillings – a three pence tip!"

I held the thrupenny piece in my hand as he walked away.

"No wonder you're a fucking millionaire, Max," and spun the piece in the air. He kept walking. I half expected him to pick it up. Despite coming from the right manor, he was definitely not 'one of our own'.

Dangerous Liaisons

One sunny day I bought a coffee and a roll, and pulled off the road in a leafy square in Paddington to have a break. I had just finished my food, when a there was a knock at the window and standing there was a blonde with a short flared ra-ra skirt and grubby blouse. I remembered her face; she tried not to pay her fare one night.

"Hello, what are you doing?" she asked in a Yorkshire accent.

"Hello, just having a break."

"Fancy a good time? It's hot today" raising her skirts to show she wasn't wearing any 'Alan Whickers'. Not a pretty sight and reminded me only that I needed to get my 'barnet' trimmed.

"Fancy coming up to the flat with me?"

The flats to my right were an old, exclusive block of flats.

Judging from her appearance, she did not belong to there. I looked at the doorway, spied a Mike Tyson lookalike and the penny dropped: get out of the cab with my money bag, enter the hallway and it would be lights out for me.

"Okay," I said, "I'll park down the square on a meter."

She walked to the entrance. I was on Paddington Station cab rank within minutes.

Notting Hill in Ladbroke Grove

Shortly after the film 'Notting Hill' came out, I was in Oxford Gardens, Ladbroke Grove. At the top was Holland Park which was quite trendy and was home to film stars and politicians; the middle part was dangerous if you were a tourist or not streetwise. It was midday, broad daylight, when a Yank with his wife ran towards the cab, being chased by four black kids, about thirteen years old, who were trying to pull the Yank's camera from him his hands. We got away despite of one the kids getting in the cab, still trying one last time to steal the camera. The Yank's wife was crying and distraught. He was shook up, to say the least.

His only error was to look for the property where the Notting Hill film was shot.

The Lavender Hill Mob of Ladbroke Grove

About 3am I was stopped while at the lights in Ladbroke Grove. It was the early nineties and the country was in recession. It meant long hours to get your living. I was finished for the night, and told him so. He asked which direction I wanted to go and then told me that was the direction he wanted to go. Alarm bells not yet ringing.

"Before you go," he said, "take me round to Chesterton Road and I'll collect some drugs and money so I can pay you."

I told him I didn't want anything to do with drugs. He went down some stairs to a basement flat, came back and said, "I haven't got enough money for the drugs. Lend me fifty quid."

I said, "Do me a favour. Just leave it out."

"Okay, just give me a minute," he said, using his mobile to make a call. About five minutes later, three heavyweights in tracksuits came around the corner of the cab.

Wake up, son! The alarm bells were loud and clear now, and my cab was away with the three big boys trying to stop me.

I found out later that a couple of cab drivers had been

conned out of money and one was beaten up. It was a regular scam in Ladbroke Grove.

Ali Baba

In the recession, you had to take what came. Maybe it wasn't what you would normally do to get a living.

I was in Portman Square, in the West End, when a very large Arab in a gown touching the floor stopped me and put cards through the window. These cards were common and the punters looking for girls found them in the telephone boxes. He had already phoned for availability and the address he gave me was in Lancaster Gate. I expected that when we got there he would pay me off. Wrong. He wanted me to go up the stairs with him to make sure he would be safe and not mugged.

Up the stairs we go, me in front. I knock and a Glaswegian madam opened the door. She could see my cab badge, which, by Hackney Carriage law, had to be worn at all times, and I pointed to Ali. We went into a small room with three doors and a sun tan machine in the corner. Ali lent against the machine and copped a full volley from the Glaswegian madam, a woman not for the faint-hearted. "Get off there, you fat bastard!"

Ali wasn't put off. He asked to see 'the girls'. Two girls, who sounded like they came from Birmingham, came out with the full kit on: stockings, basques etc. Ali asked how much and the madam asked which girl he wanted. "Both" was his reply.

Ali went in one of the rooms with the two Brummie girls.

The madam made me a cup of tea, which I had just finished together with a nice conversation with Mary the Madam (whose bark it turned out was worse than her bite) when Ali came out, red in the face. I bid the girls goodnight and went down to the cab with Ali, who produced another card with an address in Star Street, Paddington.

This time I sat outside. For about fifteen minutes, I waited, happy that the clock had been on from Portman Square and would stay on until Ali was finished for the night. Ali came out and wanted to go back to Portman Square. He paid me well, asked me to pick him up the next night at 11pm, and gave me his flat number.

The next night I was there at five minutes to eleven, rang the buzzer and asked for Ali. A female voice said, "Ali no come out tonight!"

That Ali certainly had some stamina or a pocket of Viagra!

Jack Slipper of Scotland Yard

My mother in law, Nelly, was completely unaware that some of Ronnie Biggs' haul from the Great Train Robbery had been stashed in her coal cellar. Folks in the neighbourhood acted to help their friends, and at the time, friends of Biggs might have considered it a safe hiding place. At any rate, some, such as my brother in law Michael H, paid the price with the law, despite his innocence.

I was asleep at home in Beckenham when I got an early morning call from Nelly who was very upset.

"I need your help. Micky has been arrested at his Westcliff home by Scotland Yard and he needs someone to stand bail." Out of love for Nelly, and because I liked Micky, I said I would.

I had to attend Scotland Yard and speak to Big Jack Slipper who was Ronnie Biggs' nemesis. I was shown to Slipper's office and he asked what I did for a living and stated it would be necessary for me to put my house up for bail. Knowing that Nelly had already asked her other sons-in-law, I was her last hope. I agreed, but not before speaking with Micky who gave me his assurance he would not bolt. He kept his word.

As a footnote, there was a golf match between the Sweeney, including Big Jack, and the London cab drivers. Our captain read out a made-up telegram in his afternoon speech, "Jack, sorry I couldn't be with you today. Signed, Ronnie Biggs." One half of the congregation laughed and the other half grimaced.

CHAPTER FOUR
On My Travels

I went to Philadelphia once. It was closed.
W.C. Fields

As a wedding present, my daughter Alex gave Pat and me a choice of anywhere for a long weekend. So, loving Spain, with its shops, food, and weather, we opted for Madrid. We arrived and got a cab to our hotel in the Opera district. After unpacking and a change of clothes, we went walking and were more than impressed by the high quality of the goods on display. I saw a blinding leather jacket which Pat agreed on its quality and said she would treat me to it. I said, "No rush, it's only Friday. We've got all day Saturday and Sunday to shop. Let's take it easy and chill out today". We carried on for a couple of hours window shopping and getting the lay of the land for the next day's shopping marathon.

We found a road side restaurant and sat having drinks with nuts, olives and tapas. When I asked for cigars, the waiter obliged with Romeo y Julieta. The sun was shining and we sat there watching the locals pass by for at least two hours and six drinks. We all know the measures in Spanish bars and, needless to say, we were a little 'elephants'.

We found a large piazza with some fine looking restaurants. We found one and sat down. At the next table sat a suave Spaniard, about in his late sixties, long combed back silver hair and beautiful lightweight new blue suit and plenty of jewellery dripping off his wrists. His companion was a thirty-something knock-out beautiful woman, with film star looks and figure.

I said to the missus, "she's never his wife."

"Well, he's probably twice her age but he is a suave man," she replied.

After a superb meal, and still debating the couple who had finished and left, I asked the waiter, "Are they a married couple?"

In pigeon English he replied, "No, Senor, they come here every weekend. She is lady of the night."

I can only think he must have been a wealthy man to be able to afford such a high maintenance woman.

The next day after breakfast we went to the hotel's reception.

"Excuse me, where is Madrid's best shopping area?"

In perfect English the receptionist said, "Nothing is open until Monday. It is a national holiday."

I looked at my wife's face. It was almost as if I knew and had stopped her from spending, but nothing was further from the truth.

So, we went to Madrid once. It was closed.

****

Holidays

Rover's Return Pub in Santa Ponca, Majorca
We were having a good night in the Rover's Return Pub in Santa Ponca, Majorca. The pianist was accompanying a singer from the floor; we were sitting with three couples from Glasgow, all in their late twenties and all Glasgow Rangers supporters. The door burst open and in walked an oaf with a West Ham shirt, singing something about 'Bubbles' in a loud raucous voice. I went to the bar and

ordered eight drinks for the waiter to deliver to our table. The Hammer heard my voice and in a predominantly Scottish pub said, "Oh, one of me own!"

"No, son, we are blue and white from 'over the water' and if look round at my table you'll see another three Millwall men who have copped the needle to you because of the shirt and spoiling people's entertainment with your rendition of 'Bubbles'."

The three 'Gers' were oblivious to my adopting them as Millwall supporters, as was the Happy Hammer who drank up and left.

Arenal, Majorca

In 1959 I went to Arenal, Majorca with my pal Little Jim from Peckham. We were both seventeen years old and it was our first trip on a plane to a foreign country. The main roads were normal, but the side roads were sand and stone, very primitive. At the back of the hotel was a chicken coop. We unpacked and went out to suss out the surroundings and bought a large green melon. When we got back to the room, we each had a slice of the melon. To save the rest of the melon, I filled a contraption in the bathroom with cold water and deposited the remaining half of melon.

At the dinner table we were seated with a honeymoon couple from Manchester and I naively asked him what that contraption in the bathroom was.

He whispered in my ear, "Bidet," and explained what it was used for.

That night after a night on the town, and in darkness, the melon was lobbed over the balcony rail and into the chicken coop, resulting in the chickens squawking in Spanish and our learning the continental way of cleanliness.

On the same holiday, we were drinking with two young French women. Their tipple was Pernod, which has to have liquid or water added.

My Dad told me not to drink the water in Spain, so, being a good listener, I advised Little Jim, and we both drank the Pernod neat. Needless to say, we were 'Brahms and Lizst'.

The next day we went for breakfast and then onto the beach. With the temperature in the high nineties we drank cans of Coke and were drunk again, with the Coke mixing with the Pernod inside us.

Clever people 'Les Frogs': buy a round of Pernod and get drunk twice for the price of one.

Mediterranean Cruise

Me and the missus went on a Mediterranean cruise, leaving from Palma Majorca. After unpacking our cases and having a change of clothing, we went down to the bar to relax with a nice cold drink. The ship was just leaving port as I drew my first puff on my Churchill Cohiba. A young steward came running over and rudely said, "Put that out. No cigars allowed in this bar."

"Quick! Run like fuck and tell the Captain to turn the boat around and get my cases off," I said.

"Why's that?" the young pimple-faced youth enquired.

"Because there's nothing in your brochure that states I can't smoke a cigar for the next ten days. And if there was, I wouldn't be sitting here," I said.

Pat, my missus, being the holiday booker, concurred.

The steward left the bar and an elderly passenger came up and said, "Well done. I'm also a cigar man."

For the next ten days I enjoyed a fine cigar in the bar every evening with no complaints from either passengers or crew.

Scotland to Stansted

My wife and I were at Glasgow Airport one Saturday morning in priority booking, waiting to be called for the Stansted flight. When the flight was announced, my wife was quicker to the queue than I was and in between us stepped a slim Scottish six footer in his late twenties. As I approached to re-join my wife, I had to pass the fellow, saying "Excuse me, please," at which point he grabbed my shoulder, spun me around and in a guttural Glaswegian accent growled, "Where you going?"

"I would like to stand with my wife," I replied.

"That's okay, then," he begrudgingly spat, as if he was judge and jury. Despite being sixty eight years old, the red mist descended, and I grabbed him by the throat.

"That's okay! Who the fuck do you think you are?"

Amid the disquiet of the following travellers, a representative of the airlines appeared. "Neither of you will board this plane unless you apologise to the other passengers."

Knowing that my daughter and my three grandkids were waiting to collect us at Stansted, and my wife urging me to do so, I did. As also did the long streak of piss.

"I get yous at Stansted," he growled.

"Okay by me, look forward to it," I said out of the corner of my mouth, not wanting to be seen by the airlines rep.

I got my mobile out, dialled my daughter and in a loud voice said, "When you get to the terminal bring all the boys." The tall man heard it and when we boarded the plane at the plane at the front, he went to rear. Never to be seen again.

The boys question were four and six years old.

With My Parents In St Helier, Jersey

When I was fourteen years old, my Parents and my Dad's pal Bill Simpson and I all went on holiday to St Helier in Jersey. We travelled on an overnight ferry from Southampton, and it was a very rough crossing. As it got light, we were almost there and I was on deck with my Mum who was enjoying a smoke. Suddenly from below deck my Dad appeared in a smart grey suit, not noticing the various deposits of 'Belle Vue' dotted about. He walked towards us concentrating on lighting his fag, slipping in a pile of 'Hackney Wick'. He must have slid about ten feet on his backside. Me and Mum contained our laughter, but when he wasn't looking she spoke her immortal word, "Dollop."

Bill Simpson, right, (locked in toilet), Jersey 1956

We embarked and got a 'Sandy McNab' to the guesthouse that was owned and run by an old French couple. I shared a room with Bill who was profoundly deaf and my Dad's best pal since their school days.

We had all just finished breakfast and Bill went to the bathroom for the toilet. I was in the bedroom wanting to go out, when I heard Bill calling my name and trying to get out of bathroom. The French proprietors were on the landing, banging on the door and asking Bill what was wrong. Of course, Bill was oblivious to their banging.

My Dad always carried a pencil and paper in his pocket just in case people couldn't understand him. He wrote "What's wrong, Bill?" and put both the note and the pencil under the door. Up to this point Bill wasn't aware that we were all outside the door.

Bill wrote back "I'm locked in and the key has broken in the lock."

By now the rest of the boarders were on the landing, all trying to help. Two big Scousers offered to break the door down but the elderly French couple weren't having that. My Dad put more notes under the door and Bill replied and sat on the toilet, waiting. The French lady phoned for the Fire Brigade, and they got in via the 'Tommy Trinder' saving the day.

My Mum's window summary of the events was summed up by one word: "Dollop."

Talk about a French farce!

In Paris

Pat and I went to Paris to celebrate one of her birthdays, and we got a cab from Charles de Gaulle Airport to our hotel in the Notre Dame area. I engaged the cab driver in French and he spoke pigeon English. We spoke about the cab trade and my wife was impressed at my command of the French language.

Walking around the back streets of Paris, we entered a cafe. The owner was a scruffy Parisian with a white vest (grey really), uncombed bushy hair and a hairy chest looking completely unhygienic.

I asked him where the toilet was, to which he replied in good English "Follow the flies."

He wasn't joking.

Tom Jones

Pat and I were visiting Liz and Ian in Sydney, Australia. I had never met them before, but they were old friends of Pat's and a nice couple.

On the Friday I asked if there was a club we could go to on Saturday night. Ian said that the Blacktown Working Man's Club always had entertainment. So, getting ready to go out, I asked if it was okay to wear a suit, to which Ian said yes. Pat and I both got done up as if it was a Saturday night back home. When we got to the club, it was very impressive, along the lines of Vegas, with slot machines and a large auditorium.

I noticed that people were all very casually dressed in shorts, vests and sandals. The entertainment was a Tom Jones impersonator who was receiving a mixed review.

I got up to go to the toilet and right in the middle of a nelson riddle, an elderly Aussie burst in, enquiring, "Ain't you gonna stop the fight?"

"What's it got to do with me?" I asked.

"You his manager, ain't ya?"

Apparently, Tom Jones had lost his temper with a heckler and a scuffle ensued. As I was the only person suited and booted, it was assumed I was his manager.

Iron Mike

I was stopping in the hotel opposite Madison Square Gardens – Pennsylvania 65000 – it was called after the Glen Miller record, and having breakfast with three other London cab drivers when Mike Tyson and his trainer walked past our table. We engaged him in conversation and he was quite friendly and chatty.

The next day, after his training he came past our table and stopped to talk. Someone from our party said he heard Mike was due to fight Frank Bruno. Tyson confirmed this and added, "I hear he is a very fine gentleman."

His trainer, I believe his name was Rooney, said, "He's a fucking bum."

So, as much as the London contingent loved the fellow London hopeful, this remark was greeted with stony silence. Nobody fancied a téte a téte with the future ear biting Mike and his trainer.

The next morning we were all too engrossed in our eggs and bacon to notice the duo passing through.

CHAPTER FIVE
Covent Garden Market

Covent Garden is not the oldest fruit and veg market in London. That accolade goes to Borough Market, first recorded in 1014 and located just to the south of London Bridge. Nevertheless, excavations in and around Covent Garden show human occupation as early as the seventh century.

The land that later became known as Covent Garden Market originally was owned by the monks of Westminster Abbey who used it as their kitchen garden for the needs of the monastery. Henry VIII, that much married monarch who set up the Church of England, dissolved the monasteries and appropriated the monks' garden for the Crown. Edward VI granted this area of land, along with the land now encompassing Bloomsbury, in 1552 to John Russell, first Earl of Bedford, for services to the Crown, with Covent Garden and Bloomsbury becoming what was to be known as the Bedford Estates.

Before he lost his head, Charles I granted a licence in 1630 for development of Covent Garden to the fourth Earl, Francis Russell, who commissioned Inigo Jones to design an Italian-style scheme of houses to surround the area, incorporating gardens and the beautiful piazza we see today. Covent Garden Market proper was born in 1670, by act of royal charter authorising "the buying and selling of all manner of fruits, flowers and herbs". It only made sense: at that time, within a ten-mile radius of Covent Garden there were over 15,000 acres of small kitchen gardens and smaller fruit and veg markets which could provide for the needs of the London. The fifth Earl, William Russell, obtained from Charles II the charter which permitted establishment, within the piazza, of a daily fruit and vegetable market and the collection of fees from market traders. Coupled with the growth of London in the seventeenth and eighteenth centuries as a leading world centre for merchants and enterprise, Covent Garden became the natural focus for trading, becoming, arguably, the most famous market emporium in England.

In 1918, the Duke of Bedford sold the estate to the Covent Garden Estate Company, owned by the Beecham family. By Act of Parliament in 1962, the Covent Garden Market

Authority was set up to manage it. All good things come to an end: in 1974 the life and colour of the old wholesale fruit and vegetable market was moved to Nine Elms, replaced by trendy shops, restaurants and bars so beloved of tourists to our shores.

****

When I worked in the Old Covent Garden Market it was a different world, and a whole new world for me in terms of an education in streetwise. I started as a cashier, then junior salesman on a vegetable stand and finished up with a large orange, lemon and grapefruit stand on my own.

I started at 3am and walked the market to suss out if there was a shortage of my stock, which would mean I could increase the price from the day before. If the market was inundated with a certain item, I would need to find a new price to sell at.

The pubs were open early and salesmen would take their inventory board into the pub and enjoy a rum and coffee with the head porter at the door with a pint ready to take the sales to the various lorries.

The commission agents all bought in bulk for shipping all over England and would congregate in the pubs for business.

In R.E. Jenkinson's cashiers box out of the rain, eating a sandwich

To become a market porter, you had to be recommended by a family member who was an existing porter and usually accompanied you to see the union, a three man committee. The prospective porter had to swear to be loyal to his fellow brothers and to pay his union dues promptly, after which, a market badge was issued and the new boy was allocated a company to work for.

It was a tough game and I learned several lessons the hard way. Selling too low, being conned by the agents who knew the market better than I did. You always had the fear of not shifting your stock and took a bit less to move it, and to keep in with the agents who bought in bulk, a 150 there, etc.

The worst time was in the summer and the market opened on Saturdays. In those days there was little refrigeration, and I remember I was left with strawberries that would not last until Monday. The barrow boys were there to take away bargains at the last knockings. Salesmen in desperation sold the perishables for knockdown prices, rather than throwing them away. I can still see the face of a barrow boy from Croydon market, who was as quick as a ferret and about as likeable, clearing my strawberries out to his van for peanut prices.

A young Dave Murray (Micky's brother) pulling a turn out in the sixties

In the cellars of the market were rats, mice, wild cats, tailored suits, shirts, overcoats and shoes. The rats and mice were chased by the wild cats which were fed by the porters.

The tailored suits, shirts, overcoats and shoes were on sale at half price of their labels. A porter named 'Two of Veg' (Reg) would pass my stand and out of the corner of his mouth would say "Forty two short, come to see me at your break." Talking out of the side of the mouth emanates from the prison exercise yard – no talking allowed. So at my breakfast break I would go to see Two of Veg in the cellar below the market. Apart from the dim lighting it was similar to a tailor's shop, suits hanging up, full length mirrors, and Reg with a measuring tape around his neck. "Just in last night, half price to you" Reg would say, looking at the price tag and the make. It was a bargain, straight from the top men's shops in London.

Men's clothing wasn't the only items on sale: throughout the market's cellars household goods, toys, you name it there it was. Rumour has it that some of the Great Train Robbers' cash was hidden in the cellars. Not surprising as at least three of the robbers had worked in the market.

I loved working at the market: it was an education and reminded me of Dickens' time with antiquated wooden barrows, tough raw-boned men pulling them with shirts opened to the waist in mid-winter, men carrying baskets and boxes on their heads which was a really specialised skill. Ninety percent of market workers were Cockneys and all had a good line of patter.

The salesmen and office workers made up the other ten percent and if you came from a middle class background you could find yourself all at sea with the jargon.

Prices could vary depending on the size of the purchase. As an example, the greengrocer looking for one or two items would be quoted a slightly higher price than the bulk buyer who would expect good treatment.

The figures quoted to a customer were a mish mash from racing, rhyming slang, the odd Army term or Cockney backslang – a reversal of words. To the question 'How much are those 'boy scouts' (Brussel sprouts)?' the reply might involve the following:

Ounce - one;

Deuce or bottle - two, deuce from cards;

A carpet - three, the story goes that after three years' incarceration in jail the inmate got a small mat for his cell;

A ruof - four backwards;

Jacks - five, jacks alive from cards;

Tom - six, Tom Mix the cowboy;

A neves - seven, backwards;

A th - eight, the last letters of eight backwards;

Enin - nine backwards;

A cock-and-hen - ten;

Lord of the Manor - tanner, six pence;

Joey - three penny bit;

Oxford - Oxford scholar, or dollar five shillings;

Cow's - cow's calf or half of a £1;

Apple - apple core or score, meaning £20;

Pony - £25, a racing term for the price back when for the cost of a pony;

Bullseye - £50, a term from game of darts;

One Large or a Century - £100, self-explanatory;

Monkey - £500, derived from the Indian Raj Army days when a 500 rupee note had a monkey on it.

As mentioned previously, anything could be bought in the market.

One day I was approached by a well-known 'face' called Patsy who asked if I was interested in buying a key. He said the key would open all the parking meters in Kensington and Knightsbridge! After ten seconds of conversation I turned him down. I had visions of walking lop-sided in Kensington High Street with tonness of coins in my 'sky rocket'.

Almost every day there would be a tear-up either between the porters, or porters against lorry loaders, or interlopers for early morning drinks who misbehaved. The porters believed the early pubs were exclusively for market workers and any who 'acted the goat' after a night on the town would be told were to go.

A classic was Richard Harris, a hell-raiser who was larking about drunk among the porters, received a bosh from a seventy year old and was slung through the pub doors into Bow Street.

Back then there were no calculators so mental arithmetic, or the side of a cardboard orange box, came in handy to enable you to write out your sales ticket. The former was something that stood me in good shape for my last occupation.

There were many scams operational back then, and I can only recount one such folly which was very profitable. When a shipment arrived by boat sometimes the goods were showing 'wets' or goods that had gone off. But they still had to be sold.

For example, oranges were packed in cardboard containers and the bad ones showed wet on the outside. So the night foreman would pack the oranges ten by ten in a large square, putting the wets on the outside, thus giving the impression that all the stock was bad. The salesman would phone the representative of the sender as soon as possible, before the market got busy, usually about 3.30am, and inform him about the state of the newly-arrived stock. The sender's representative would then come down and inspect the outside of the cardboard boxes where the wets were showing, and satisfied that the all stock was bad, would instruct the salesman to sell at, say, ten shillings a box, a vastly reduced price from the closing prices of the day before. The representative, wanting the supposed poor shipment with his brand name on out of the way, gave the salesman one price to clear all the boxes of stock, *despite the fact that the fruit in the middle of the boxes was as good as gold.*

The knowledgeable salesman knew all the barrow boys who dealt big and would take the lot away at a good price for them. He would phone a team of brothers who had stalls all over central London, and they would arrive tout suite. The barrow boys, realising a bargain was there for the taking, would bid for the lot. For example, if the representative had fixed a price of ten shillings a box, and the previous days' prices were two pound-odd, the salesman would quote £1 a box to the barrow boys, which, after much haggling the price, was agreed. This left ten shillings a box to be shared among the night foreman, the salesman and the cashier. Back then, a nice little earner!

I was never bold enough to dabble, but I admired the ingenuity shown as related to me by the drunken salesman early one morning in the early pubs.

The market had more than its fair share of hard men and villains. One story to illustrate will suffice. It was a wintery Friday and the market was closing down for the weekend. I was at the coffee stall with my good pal, Micky Murray, having a cup of tea and a bacon roll. I had my cotchel (fruit and veg) and Micky, who worked in the flower market, had flowers for his mother. A very attractive redhead walked past with an older man in a large overcoat and trilby hat. She smiled and we both acknowledged her. Her companion was not pleased.

"I'll deal with you pair of mugs later," he snarled, obviously very annoyed.

Micky, all five foot seven and ten stone of him soaking wet, responded, by saying to me, "Hold my flowers," in readiness for a tear-up. Micky had a low golf handicap and was a very talented footballer, but with all due respect, he was not in the top class when it came to fisticuffs.

"Leave it, Micky," I said and was glad to see the 'ice cream' walk away. It transpires that he had just come out after doing ten years, so we didn't know who he was. The redhead was his daughter, and he took umbrage at our smiling at her. He was also not averse to shooting people that vexed him. A good friend put me in the picture about the guy, telling me his history, and suggested me and Micky make ourselves scarce for a while, as he was looking for us.

The market had a massive underground toilet with many traps. I popped into one of these, with Micky next door. Every so often, he would whisper, "Do you think it's safe yet?" After about forty five minutes, we came up for air and made a quick getaway.

The story had an unhappy ending for our chaser. Unfortunately, he was the victim of a hit and run accident, and was killed a few weeks later on a busy south-east London street.

Even today, forty four years later, whenever I mention his initials to Micky, he still shakes his head, thinking how lucky he was that I didn't 'hold his flowers'.

The market was a male preserve and any lady walking through was treated royally. The wife of a good friend of mine walked through the market every day and, apart from the wolf whistles, she was always assisted with heavy bags of shopping.

In a way the market could be compared to the Stock Exchange where daddy would recommend son and heir. Most porters were put forward by family to the union to be vetted, and in my time the union man was Harry Loomes, a great guy and I enjoyed his company. I had taken a correspondence course at Ruskin College on trade unionism and got my certificate. In Harry's company I learned a lot that would stand me in good stead later in life.

My good pal Micky Murray left London in the seventies to go to Canada. He had no trade; he was a Covent Garden porter from Del Boy land of Peckham. He went to night school, got a job with Arrow, the shirt manufacturer, and never looked back. He was their buyer in Asia and retired recently, quite well-heeled.

Micky gave me a story that he was proud of: one day he was invited to play golf in a foursome at Coombe Hill, Surrey. The guy who invited him said he had a surprise playing partner. When they got on the tee it was none other than 007 himself: Sean Connery.

Micky took ten shillings off 007 and was invited back to his house to play snooker which having a misspent youth at Peckham Billiard Hall doubled to £1.

Micky said to me 'Who'd have thought a market porter from Peckham would be hobnobbing with film stars'.

Micky is not an isolated case, many Londoners have made a good life for themselves, built upon their personality and street nouse.

****

Market Characters

Charlie Powell

The Old Covent Garden Market was full of scams, skulduggery and real life. The perfect school for a street education. And it was also full of characters, one of which was the bold Charlie Powell.

When I was a salesman Charlie was one of my porters. For about three days on the spin he would say 'Watch this'. Every morning about 7am a green grocer would race through the market with three punnets of mushrooms on each arm, eager to get them to his shop. Charlie would step out from behind boxes with a fag in his mouth and ask the greengrocer for a light. The greengrocer would oblige and put his six boxes on the floor and light Charlie up. On the third day the penny dropped that little Charlie was taking the mickey, and the greengrocer gave chase. Charlie made himself scarce after that.

Billy Gilmore
One of my fellow salesmen was another young man in his early twenties, Billy Gilmore. When we had a good morning Bill and I would get a cab to Knightsbridge and have breakfast at the Rib Room at the Carlton Tower Hotel. This was the other end of the market and when we walked in the head waiter would look us up and down, the suits and shirts were fine but the dirty Chelsea boots and the trousers turned up from the market's grime was the giveaway. But it was okay as we always tipped well.

In the early sixties I had an overcoat made in Deptford by a man who went on to be the tailor for the stars in Mayfair. This overcoat cost me a pony. It really was the business: guards back, a pleat between the shoulders, heavy Crombie material, double-breasted, with a top pocket for the silk handkerchief. I sold it to Billy in the late sixties for the same price I bought it at. Billy was happy.

An old market man told me in 2005 that Billy still wears that coat in the winter along with his pork pie hat. Good quality always lasts. Is forty-three years to wear a garment something the Guinness Book of Records should know?

Jimmy Mott

Another character was the King of cockney rhyming slang, Jimmy Mott. The story goes that when Prince Charles was in his teens he would visit the market in the wee small hours with his minders. Jimmy, who was never a shrinking violet, would seat Charles on an orange box, make tea for his party, and teach 'One' rhyming slang. I doubt if Her Majesty was aware, and would loved to have known if Charles practised on Philip.

A conversation with Jimmy one morning went along the lines of "I took the 'jam jar' (car) in for a 'Brian Curvis' (service), they changed the 'Jack Doyle' (oil), took up the 'Hattie Jacques' (brakes) and told me it needed a 'Cassius Clay'" (spray).

Jimmy was a good singer which I witnessed at a 'moriarty' one night and a born comedian. One of the worst jobs for a porter was to take a barrow load of potatoes up the hill to Long Acre: "Morning, Jim. How goes it?"

"I've been up that fucking hill more times than the Grand Old Duke of York!"

Joe Da Costa

The market boasted numerous characters, none more so than Joe Da Costa the commission agent. A commission agent bought in bulk and shipped out to various parts of England and was always looking for the most competitive rate. To shift his stock, the salesman had to oblige the commission agents by giving them cheaper rates for bulk, so the agents were big shots in the market. And none more so than Joe Da Costa.

Joe was a big man and immaculately dressed, but not in the conventional style. If he chose green, he wore a green three-piece tailored suit, a matching bowler hat and green suede shoes.

Every suit I saw – and I saw several – had a bowler hat to match: red, blue, green, brown, and he always strolled about with a rolled umbrella.

In the market he cut an imperious figure, seldom smiling. He could be quite intimidating for young salesmen. After doing a deal with Joe, you knew he had 'legged you over' and had to make better prices with the remaining stock.

When the porters saw him coming, they would hide behind the stack of boxes and give him some stick. Green suit and they would sing Robin Hood. Red suit and some line about a moving letterbox and so on.

Joe never really let his guard down and there were few people who knew him very well, so he remained aloof, which suited his persona.

George Scott

Another character was George Scott, an East Ender who at one time ran the Covent Garden football team. He had been a sergeant major in the army and was a typical rough, blunt market porter who I loved to talk to. Everybody was called 'laddie' from his army days, and he cut an impressive figure at about nineteen stone of bulk.

He was a Spurs supporter and on Monday he would ask if I had been to Millwall last Saturday and a typical conversation would be along the lines of the following:

'Was it a good game, laddie?' he would enquire. 'Well, we lost 2-1, hit the post twice and had a blatant penalty turned down', making all the excuses for getting beat. 'What was the score in The News of the World yesterday, laddie?'

'1–2' I replied. End of conversation. I could always imagine George on the wall at Rorke's Drift controlling the lads.

Unfortunately, Old Covent Garden Market died when it transferred to Nine Elms in 1974 and automation came in with forklifts and modernisation. By then I had done the Knowledge and had become a licensed London Taxi Driver.

CHAPTER SIX
The Knowledge

I was fed up getting out of bed at 2am and going to bed in the afternoon for a couple of hours, and then having no night life because of getting to bed at 10pm. If you had the flu, you had broken sleep and it lasted ages. I had a friend of a friend that had driven a cab for several years and he wore only the best clothes, dined in the best restaurants and had good holidays. I asked him if he made a living. "I get a crust," he said. That was good enough for me.

The passion I had to learn about the greatest city in the world was reflected by the short time it took me to learn the nooks and crannies. I already knew east and south-east London, and I had a good handle on the West End from my clubbing and shopping days. I was at a loss with north London and west London, so that's where I concentrated. I went to the places I had never been to before: The Bishop's Avenue aka Millionaire's Row; Hampstead Heath and the suburbs: Chiswick Village, Kew, Highgate Hill, Acton, Ealing and Golders Green.

I borrowed Micky Murray's moped. It was the Harley Davidson of mopeds: big handle bars shaped in a large V. I fixed my board between the V to attach my Blue Book runs for my routes.

The Blue Book, originally blue but now white, had runs on each page. These runs were not in any order, so to save wasting time you picked five runs a day that followed on from each other. Eventually the penny dropped and as you reached a crossroad, you said to yourself 'That's the road I took to X'. All the runs criss-crossed London.

I loved it; no helmets in those days. Straight leg Levis, a Fred Perry three-button polo shirt in the summer and a blinding 'Charlie Chan' as a bonus. In the winter it was a different story: cheese cutter cap with a button on top, a thick 'pint and half', football socks and an all-encompassing oilskin coat that reached the ankles which caused a little Sloanie to say to his mother "Oh, look mother, it's the man from Chitty Chitty Bang Bang".

I was comfortable on the moped until I reached Marble Arch and Hyde Park Corner, where there were no traffic lights. It was dog eat dog. I waited for a bus to come along and appended myself as close to the conductor on the platform as physically possible until I was safe in Park Lane.

On the runs you left space in the margins to write down places of interest, big offices, theatres, cinemas, embassies etc. and whether on the left or right hand side of the road.

The key for me was to lie in bed last thing at night, eyes closed – no, not thinking of Bardot or Monroe – but 'seeing' the roads and turns where I had been that day. The next day the run was firmly in my mind.

In the beginning you made an appearance once a month at the Public Carriage Office at Penton Street, the Angel, Islington. All this was after your past had been checked for any criminal record and your 'kipper and bloater' taken.

I put on the full monty: my best three-piece suit, large white handkerchief in top pocket, shoes gleaming, white shirt, silk tie and hair in a short Perry Como – the image the PCO wanted. All the Knowledge boys were put into a waiting room, not knowing what to expect, but all having heard about 'the Scotsman'.

At the time there were four examiners, all of them ex-police sergeants.

Mr Wicks had the best knowledge of London of anybody alive. He could be seen cycling about on a Sunday morning in khaki shorts looking for 'Jekyll and Hyde' questions to ask us lambs to the slaughter. My finest hour with him was when he asked me at an appearance 'Where is the Spiritualist Society of Great Britain?' As quick as a flash I said '33 Belgrave Square, Sir'. The 'Sir' was obligatory.

'What colour is the letterbox, Mr Lewis?'

'Can I crack a joke, Sir?'

'Yes, Mr Lewis.'

'I was hoping to be a cab driver, not a postman, Sir.'

He smiled, and as a punishment for my cheek, asked me to name all blocks of flats from Lambeth Town Hall to the top of Brixton Hill. I started off with Wavertree and finished with 'I'm not certain if the last one is Dumbarton or Dunfermline, Sir'.

'Very good, Mr Lewis. It won't be long before you get your badge.' And, I'm pleased to say, it wasn't.

Stuck in traffic one day in Bond Street, an elderly cab driver said to me 'Turn it in, son. It takes a lot of brains to pass the

Knowledge.' I replied 'You don't exactly look like Bamber Gascoigne. Did the PCO take pity on you?'

Mr Miller was a PCO examiner and a gentleman. Rumour had it that he lost his leg while pursuing bank robbers in south-east London as a police motor bike rider. There was no side to him; he was always polite and cheerful.

Mr Rance was also a gentleman and gave me good advice one day. "When you get your cab licence, don't think the Knowledge is over. At the traffic lights when you stop, look around you and look for more knowledge." He then put me to the test. "You are sitting by the lights at Lambeth North tube station. What can you see?" As luck would have it, I travelled home every day from the market via Lambeth North. "Yes Sir. Floods Estate Offices, Lambeth Building Society, the Hercules Pub."

"Very good" he said and gave me a reduction to three weeks which meant 'appearing' every three weeks instead of four. I was on my way.

Always save the best until last. 'The Scotsman', Mr Finlay was the temperament tester. He was there solely to see if you would lose your 'filbert'. When he came to the waiting room door and called your name, I've seen the toughest guys shuffle their feet with apprehension and a few trousers change colour.

"Mr Lewis, this way laddie." We were all called 'laddie' even if you were elderly.

When you walked into his office, he sat behind the desk and you gave him your appointment card and walked back to the chair in isolation in the middle of the room. If you sat down he would bark "Who told you to sit down, laddie?"

"Sorry, Sir."

"Sit."

At that time all runs had to be called orally. For example, say it was Savoy Hotel to Paddington Station. "Leave it on the left in the Strand, forward Charing Cross, convey the one way system Trafalgar Square, leave by Admiralty Arch, forward The Mall, convey one way system Queen Victoria Memorial, leave by Constitutional Hill etc. etc."

With all the examiners, it was never easy. They would ask five or six runs and mark you accordingly. They wouldn't ask big landmarks, so when you were on your bike you took a penny and drew a circle around your start and finish point on the map, and took in all the surrounding streets. So, as with the above example of Savoy Hotel to Paddington Station, it would more likely be Coutts Bank to Eastbourne House. You really had to mop up streets and points. Points are places of interest and importance.

Anyway, back to the Scotsman, or as some of the less knowledgeable would say 'the Scotchman'. When asked to call a run, I would shut my eyes so I could 'see' it. It helped not to see him because he would walk the window, lift his jacket over his head and wiggle his 'plaster' from left to right. Or he would throw all his pencils up in the air and look for a reaction. If you laughed and stopped calling the run, he would say "What have you stopped for, laddie? If a passenger spilt his briefcase in the back of the cab, would you stop in the middle of Marble Arch?"

"No sir."

"Then get on with it."

He tested me one day with Endymion Road to Endymion Road. One was off Brixton Hill and the other in Tottenham, probably ten miles apart. It was not a run he expected me to be able to do. Both the streets were not big and not well known. He told me to come back in two weeks. I was nearly there!

There are lots of stories about Mr Finlay. He was a legend. Although many of the Knowledge boys were in fear of him, if he thought you were working at it, he would mark you high.

An example was when a Knowledge boy came off his bike in the ice and broke his arm. The Scotsman asked what had happened and told him to get out and stop wasting his time. At his next appearance the examiner said that Mr Finlay was pleased with him and had given him full marks.

A black Knowledge boy was fed up with Mr Finlay and told him he was a racist and that he was going to report him to the Race Relations Board. The Scotsman sat there deadpan and said "Okay, laddie, one last chance. Take me from here to the Race Relations Board." The Knowledge boy said "I don't know where it is!"

"Get out laddie and stop wasting my time." He retorted.

One day a candidate lost his temper and punched Mr Finlay who just stood up and tore up the guy's appointment card.

As a footnote to Mr Finlay, when he died his funeral was well-attended by the London cab trade.

When you were on two-week appearances, and got the much-awaited stations, you knew that was it. It was good old Mr Finlay that asked me to call Euston Station to Paddington Station, Paddington Station to Victoria, Victoria to Liverpool Street and finally Fulham Football Club to Orient Football Club. He stood up and said "No more London Knowledge for you, laddie. Now the suburbs and a driving test." I walked forward to thank and shake hands with him.

Nine and a half months. A record.

But no mistake, I did six hours a day after leaving the market at midday. The suburbs were a piece of cake. You only needed to know how to get from central London out to all points of the compass. We were Green Badges. In the outlying districts were Yellow Badges, who were only allowed to work their own areas: Croydon, Ilford etc.

The Drive, as it was called, might have proved tricky because of my lack of experience behind the wheel of a cab. A three-point turn between cones in the PCO yard, then hold the cab on a hill with the hand brake off, and then a drive through London traffic with an examiner in the back.

It had all started in August 1968. By April 1969, I had my badge and licence – Number 16320. I was twenty-seven years old. All I had to do now was get a living.

****

London

Everyone believes they know their city. I thought I did until I completed the Knowledge of London. Once I parked the moped for the final time, I realised just how much I had discovered about the hidden treasures in London's Pandora's Box.

As an example, just off Piccadilly there is an exclusive housing complex with a few houses, complete with front gardens and security to prevent Joe Public wandering through. It runs from Piccadilly through to Burlington Gardens and is **THE** place to live. I delivered a package there once and never knew of its existence.

Of course, it is a millionaire's preserve called Albany and runs parallel to the Burlington Arcade, a fantastic pedestrian shopping arcade. There are bollards at either end because, in June 1954, a gang drove a Jaguar car after 'doing' the Goldsmiths and the Silversmiths Associations' windows, and getting away with £40,000 worth of goods.

Across the road in Piccadilly are two other arcades: Piccadilly Arcade and Prince's Arcade that specialise in unusual upmarket items such as cuff links, military ties and waistcoats.

Jermyn Street

Jermyn Street runs parallel to Piccadilly and is my favourite shopping street in London. It caters mainly for men, and there are shoe, shirt, and suit outfitters where items are made of the finest quality materials.

At the St James end of Jermyn Street is the cigar smoker's dream: Davidoffs.

All of the above are within walking distance of Piccadilly Circus and are at the top end of the market for those who like to dress with some 'Tate and Lyle'. As a footnote to Piccadilly, an old cab driver told me that when a policeman was nicking him for illegal parking, he asked the officer if he was the one who found a dead horse in Piccadilly and being unable to spell 'Piccadilly' for his notebook he pulled the horse around the corner to Air Street!

St Mary-le-Bow, Bow Bells

There is a popular misconception that the Bow Bells are in Bow E3. The actual bells are in Cheapside in the City of

London, and true Cockneys need to be born with within the sound of the bells. The best time to listen for them is on Sundays when there is very little traffic in the City.

How did the word Cockney come into being? It derives from the fourteenth century Middle English word 'cokeney', literally a cock's egg, coken being the plural of 'cok plus 'ey', the Middle English for 'egg'. It was a term for the misshapen eggs laid by young hens, also used by country folk to describe townspeople ignorant of country ways. It is ironic that down the centuries Londoners reversed the thinking that country folk were not as sharp, calling them country bumpkins or swede bashers.

The Tower of London
With its ravens and Beefeaters, otherwise known as the Yeomen Warders, the Tower, lying on the north side of the River Thames was begun as a fortress by William the Conqueror in 1178 and completed by Edward I some two hundred years later. Although the Tower has served as records office, palace and mint, it is notorious as a prison wherein its first prisoner was the Bishop of Durham in 1101, and its last the Kray Twins who were stationed there in 1954 for their National Service before going awol, and

were shipped off to Shepton Mallet military prison for desertion. Just "going home for a cuppa with mum!" in their words.

The River Thames

Named Tamesis by Julius Caesar, the Thames flows eastwards 210 miles from its source in the Cotswolds, bisecting London into north and south banks, through the Thames Estuary into the North Sea. Sixty five miles of the river are tidal.

London itself evolved from a small port settlement, Londinium, on the banks where roads converged at the single point where the underlying sediments permitted the Romans to construct a viable bridge, from Southwark on the South Bank to the opposite shore. The oldest existing bridge is Westminster.

Number One London, Apsley House and the Tyburn Tree

Situated at the north side of Hyde Park Corner, the address of Apsley House is Number one London, home to the Duke of Wellington. At the other end of London's largest royal park is Speaker's Corner, close to Marble Arch, where would be politicians and cranks get on soap boxes and spout their views to anyone who cares to listen.

Around the corner, a stone in the traffic island between Bayswater Road and Edgeware Road commemorates the Tyburn Tree, the triangular shaped gallows where, from 1388 to 1783, hangings as public holiday spectacle took place. The condemned, wearing their finest clothes, travelled from Newgate Prison down what is now Oxford Street, in open carts to the cheers and jeers of crowds of sometimes up to 200,000.

By the end of the eighteenth century British jurisprudence recognised that neither the Black Laws, which gave rise to the view "as well to be hanged for a sheep as a lamb", nor 400 years' sight of their fellow men, women and children dangling from the end of a rope had much of a deterrent effect on criminal activity. Indeed the size of the crowds encouraged a thriving opportunity for gainful pick-pocketing! Tyburn gallows was dismantled but the hangings continued, removed to the more private confines of Newgate Prison until hanging was abolished for murder in 1965 (1973 in Northern Ireland), and under any circumstances (i.e. treason) in 1998.

The Savoy Hotel

The Savoy Hotel on the Strand boasts the only street in Great Britain where you are allowed to drive on the wrong side of the road. Because of its narrow forecourt, it is easier to come in on the right and exit on the left.

Dirty Dicks, 202 Bishopsgate EC2

Opposite Liverpool Street Station and a couple of doors down from Bishopsgate Police Station is a pub that always intrigued me. It opened in 1804 and given the nickname of a previous owner called Nathaniel Bentley. On the eve of his wedding, his fiancée died and Nathaniel refused to wash and lived in filth. The remains of his wedding bash, dead cats and all, were on show in the pub until the 1980s when the health department ordered a tidy up.

The Monument, Fish Hill, EC3

At 202 feet high, the Monument remains the tallest isolated stone structure in the world, designed by Sir Christopher Wren and Robert Hooke to commemorate the Great Fire of London in 1666. It has 311 steps and stands seventy-odd yards from where the fire started in Pudding Lane. It is also on the spot where it is believed the Romans came ashore.

The Great Fire helped to rid the City of the conditions responsible for the outbreak of Bubonic Plague the previous year, but also destroyed most of the City, St Paul's Cathedral and old London Bridge.

There is something about sixty-six which keeps cropping up in English history: 1066 the Battle of Hastings; 1666 the Great Fire of London; and 1966 the greatest and possibly the only time ever the Three Lions will win the World Cup (apologies to my Scottish friends).

220 | TALES FROM THE RANKS AND BEYOND

METROPOLITAN POLICE
Public Carriage Office
LIST OF QUESTIONS

similar to those put to applicants for Licences to act as CAB DRIVERS at examinations held to test their knowledge of London.

LONDON
PRINTED BY THE RECEIVER FOR THE METROPOLITAN POLICE DISTRICT
NEW SCOTLAND YARD, LONDON, SW1H 0BG
1984

LIST No. 1—ROUTES

1. Manor House Station, to Gibson Square.
2. Myddleton Square, to Golden Square.
3. Half Moon Street, W.1, to Fairhazel Gardens.
4. York Gate, Regent's Park, to Hyde Park Gardens.
5. Ladbroke Square, to Queen's Club Ground.
6. Ormonde Gate, to Kensington Town Hall.
7. Burton Court, to Bolingbroke Hospital.
8. Clapham Junction Stfl., to Imperial War Museum.
9. Thames House, S.W., to Lansdowne Club.
10. Adelphi Theatre, to Sydney Street, Chelsea.
11. Spanish Embassy, to Lambeth County Court.
12. Rotherhithe Police Station, to the Grocers Hall Court.
13. Bucklersbury, to Belgrave Hospital for Children.
14. Camberwell Green Magistrates' Court, to Lincolns Inn Fields.
15. Downing Street, to Clarence Gate, Regent's Park.
16. Belsize Park Stn., to Northern Polytechnic.
17. Oakley Square, to Portman Square.
18. Gray's Inn, to Victoria Park.

LIST No. 26—ROUTES

1. Ravenscourt Park, to Gwendolen Avenue, S.W.15.
2. Stafford Court, W.8, to Dover House Road.
3. Manor Fields, to Bedford Hill.
4. Melton Court, to Southfields Stn.
5. Vauxhall Bridge, to Dulwich College.
6. Nightingale Lane, to Honor Oak Park.
7. Waterloo Stn., to Brockley Rise.
8. Newington Butts, to Camberwell New Cemetery.
9. Clapham Police Stn., to Village Way.
10. Ludgate Circus, to Royal Circus.
11. Albert Bridge, to Streatham Common.
12. Carlyle Square, to Streatham Cemetery.
13. White City, to Sutherland Grove.
14. Primrose Hill, to Queen's Park.
15. Queen's Gate, to Chevening Road.
16. Highbury Corner, to Hampstead Heath Stn.
17. Colville Square, to Hampstead Way.
18. St. John's Way, to Woodstock Avenue, N.W.11.

TALES FROM THE RANKS AND BEYOND | 221

Metropolitan Public Carriage Act, 1869 (32 & 33 Vict., c.115)

MOTOR CAB-DRIVER'S LICENCE

No. 16320

I, having been appointed by the Secretary of State to grant cab-drivers' licences under the Metropolitan Public Carriage Act, 1869, hereby license

Roger Ivan Lewis

residing at 45 Knapmill Road, Catford, SE 6

New Address

to drive motor cabs.

This licence is granted subject to compliance by the licensee with the provisions of
    (a) the Metropolitan Public Carriage Act, 1869, and the London Cab and Stage Carriage Act, 1907, and any Order made thereunder by the Secretary of State relating to motor cab-drivers, including any regulations contained in such Order, and
    (b) the Acts relating to hackney carriages in force at the time of the commencement of the Metropolitan Public Carriage Act, 1869.

This licence shall have effect as from 10th March 1969 and shall remain in force for three years from that date unless sooner revoked or suspended.

Photograph of Licensee

Assistant Commissioner of Police of the Metropolis

Date of Issue 10 MAR 1969

Signature of Licensee

FEE 3/-

CHAPTER SEVEN
Cab Driving: A Noble Profession

My First Job

When you first get your Green Badge, the older drivers called you 'Butter Boy'. Two explanations: back when there was a general strike, grocer boys did the Knowledge and were labelled butter boys. The more likely explanation is "he is but a boy" which was certainly true in my case.

After getting my Green Badge I faced an ordeal that terrified me. How would I do when my very first fare got into my cab? Would I know where they wanted to go? Would I go the way they expected? After all, London is a massive place. Could I really be expected to know it all, I asked myself, feeling vulnerable.

It was a Thursday evening about 6pm when I left the London General Cab Company at the Oval. I didn't have the confidence to put on my 'for hire' sign straightaway. I naively thought I would work in the City of London where I prided myself on having a good knowledge. Did I really believe the job would stay in the Square Mile?

I went over Southwark Bridge and boldly put the light on. It didn't take long for a hand to go up. I was just past St Paul's Underground Station, when a smartly dressed lady in her fifties leaned in the luggage window and said, "Loudoun Road, please driver." Not a clue as to the area. She was obviously a regular cab passenger and expected me to know. After all, I was a London cabbie.

I did, in fact, know the road: it was in the vicinity of Finchley Road, in St John's Wood. She sat back and read her evening paper and I began to plot my route. There was no conversation between us, and I was pleased about this as it allowed me to concentrate on getting it perfect. We arrived and she was taken aback when I declined her money. Back then, it was considered good luck for your cab driving career to give the first job free of charge. She proffered her payment twice and I adamantly declined. So she wished me good luck, and I was never intimidated by a hand going up again.

For the first couple of weeks until the novelty wore off, I would lie in bed and recount every job on a nightly basis.

I loved the freedom of driving a cab. I was my own man. When I got into town, I would head for a station that always had a taxi rank, and away I would go. But make no mistake; driving a cab is a tough game, but also a noble profession, testing your knowledge every single day. In my day your apprenticeship was usually sixteen months, depending on how much effort was put in and much your memory could retain. Today an apprenticeship is possibly twenty four to thirty months.

After serving my apprenticeship on the Knowledge, I needed to get a living. By 1973, I had a wife and two kids to support and couldn't afford to be lax and not make provisions; the priorities being cab, mortgage payments and food. The only unknown element was illness – no work, no income.

Every day when I pulled the cab out of the garage, I had a specific amount of earnings in mind and I never went home until I reached my target. Before I went to work I wrote down everything I needed to take that day. For example, diesel, five cigars, cab repayments divided by twenty days a month, a meal with the boys, cab repairs put aside daily, holiday money, the missus' housekeeping, weekly bank deposits for the mortgage and electricity etc. All this was done daily. When I got home I took the monthly and weekly payments and put them under a pile of folded jumpers in my wardrobe until payment days. My daily system was simple: all of the above-mentioned expenses were totalled and split into four columns with equal amounts so that I was satisfied I had covered all bills. I never saw anyone else that adopted my system of calculating takings.

I used the method for two reasons: it kept my arithmetic going, which I needed after working the market, and it told me what I had to take on a fare to fare basis. Of course, today you can press a button on the 'Hickory' and it gives a running total, but not in the sixties. When the first job got out and paid a 'Lady Godiva', I knocked off the amount off the first line. I always knocked off the fare from the biggest amount column. It told me by adding the four lines up what was left before I could turn it in, more to the point it kept my arithmetic going, as did adding up the number plate of the car in front.

Today, when I teach a class to the would-be licensed drivers at the Edinburgh Taxi School (owned and run by my old pal Jim Kerlin and his lovely wife Margaret), I try to impart the importance of not over-committing yourself. To total all your financial commitments for the month, divide by four (although there are mostly five weeks) and then divide into five days. Try to get all your overheads in within five days; if you are short, there are always two more days. Under no circumstances divide by seven days because there ain't eight days in a week and you are under the cosh.

The only way to drive a cab is to be in your comfort zone, knowing you've set your financial stall out and it's achievable. Chasing money is disastrous. At the last recession there were several suicides in the London trade, mainly younger cab drivers who were living the good life – new cab, a big mortgage, HPs to the hilt. They were giving their families the best they could, working seven days and long hours. Depression set in when they realised that they couldn't pull up their commitments every week, leaving very sad families behind.

I bought my first cab for £1,871 and changed them every three years. It was a great feeling to be an owner, and I had some private clients who went every week to either Gatwick or Heathrow on business. It was money in the bank every week and, as the old saying goes, a bird in the hand etc. etc.

MANN & OVERTON LIMITED.
HIRE PURCHASE AGREEMENT

SCHEDULE

HIRER
Surname: LEWIS
Christian Names: ROGER IVAN
Address: 37, GROVELAND ROAD, BECKENHAM, KENT.

GOODS
Make and Type: AUSTIN TAXICAB Reg. No. HGX 934K Chassis Frame No. FX4/D/R20572X
Date of 1st Registration: MAY, 1972 New or Second Hand: NEW

The Hirer and Witness(es) must initial all alterations and amendments

PERIOD AND TERMS OF HIRE

Cash Price ... £1612.00	Cash Price ... £1612.00
Hiring Charges ... £ 258.00	Less Initial Instalment of Rental ... £ 466.00
Option to Purchase Fee ... £ 1.00	£1146.00
TOTAL Hire Purchase Price ... £1871.00	Add Hiring Charges ... £ 258.00
	Balance of Hire ... £1404.00

To be paid by 36 monthly instalments of ... £ 39.00
_____ monthly instalments of ... £ .
on the 24 day of each month commencing JUNE 19 72

STATUTORY NOTICE
RIGHT OF HIRER TO TERMINATE AGREEMENT

Insert one-half of hire purchase price.

1. The Hirer may put an end to his agreement by giving notice of termination in writing to any person who is entitled to collect or receive the hire rent.

2. He must then pay any instalments which are in arrear at the time when he gives notice. If when he has paid those instalments the total amount which he had paid under the agreement is less than £ 935.50 *he must also pay enough to make up that sum, unless the Court determines that a smaller sum would be equal to the Owners loss.

3. If the Goods have been damaged owing to the Hirer having failed to take reasonable care of them, the Owners may sue him for the amount of the damage unless that amount can be agreed between the Hirer and the Owners.

4. The Hirer should see whether this agreement contains provisions allowing him to put an end to the agreement on terms more favourable to him than those just mentioned. If it does he may put an end to the agreement on those terms

Insert one-third of hire purchase price.

RESTRICTION OF OWNERS RIGHT TO RECOVER GOODS

1. After £ 623.67 †has been paid, then, unless the Hirer has himself put an end to the agreement, the Owners of the Goods cannot take them back from the Hirer without the Hirer's consent unless the Owners obtain an order of the Court.

2. If the Owners apply to the Court for such an order the Court may if the Court thinks it just to do so allow the Hirer to keep either:—
   (a) The whole of the Goods, on condition that the Hirer pays the balance of the price in the manner ordered by the Court; or
   (b) A fair proportion of the Goods having regard to what the Hirer has already paid.

THE HIRER DECLARES AND ACKNOWLEDGES THAT:—

1. He accepts delivery of the Goods specified in the Schedule having examined them and satisfied himself as to their order and condition.
2. He has effected the insurance of the Goods as agreed.
3. He has already seen a written statement of the price of the Goods corresponding precisely to that shown in the schedule.
4. His express attention has been called to and he understands clauses 3 & 4 of this Agreement.

Signature of Hirer _____

Witness Signature _____
Address _____
Occupation _____

Signed for and on behalf of MANN & OVERTON LTD.

This document contains the terms of a hire-purchase agreement. Sign it only if you want to be legally bound by them.

Signature of Hirer _____

The goods will not become your property until you have made all the payments. You must not sell them before then.

Learning where to go to pick up work eventually fell into place. At the end of the week my takings were nearly always near enough the same: good days in the summer and bad days in the winter. You became a squirrel, putting your nuts away in the summer ready for a poor winter.

When I left home for work, I needed to feel good for my day's graft. The cab had to be clean and smelling nice; I had to be well turned out. In the summer I liked a nice shirt with two top pockets: one for the 'cow calfs' and £1, the other for higher values. In the winter it was a suede jacket, a cardigan or a sheepskin, and a roll neck. This was essential as I always drove with my window half down to let out the smoke.

I lived in Beckenham in Kent and it was eight miles or twenty minutes to the Oval where I usually picked up my first job. I never picked my work; wherever they wanted, they went, even if it meant going back into areas that were not cab oriented, and coming back into town empty.

I tried every different set of hours, usually to fit in with my family or branch meetings of the Association. When my kids were not old enough for school, I went out at 4am and was home about lunchtime to play with the kids in the garden. When they went to school I dropped them off and did day work and was home for 8pm for my dinner and to tuck them in until they didn't want me to. When they were teenagers I did night work and often annoyed my daughter by being outside the club when she came out to make sure she and her pals all got home safe.

There was never a better feeling for me when I was driving home with my money taken plus a good start for tomorrow, £20 or so in front. Going home after your money was taken was decided by where you were. As an example, if I was near south-east London, it was good night Vienna. But if I was in north London I would try to get near any of the eleven bridges leading home: Tower, London, Southwark, Blackfriars, Waterloo, Westminster, Lambeth, Vauxhall, Chelsea, Albert and Battersea. Incidentally, when learning the order of the bridges the last three had the initials CAB. The next two bridges – Wandsworth and Putney – were too far down for me to make my way home.

My sure fire way of getting a job home was to get in the Aldwych where the right hand side of the Church of St Mary Le Strand went only down the Strand or up towards Holborn. The left hand side of the church was a channel only leading to Waterloo Bridge and south east London.

For some reasons, there is a popular saying in the London trade "This cab don't go to south London, guv". The south London drivers were made of stronger stuff and knew the bad parts well. So when it came to going home time after the theatres and pubs turned out, there were always mobs wanting to go the route down past the left side of the Church.

For those in the wrong place, it was easy to explain "For me to get back, using the other side of the Church, I've got to go over Waterloo Bridge until the roundabout the other side, and back over the bridge again to come back here again." Ninety nine percent did not get in the cab. Only the really desperate did. So keeping left you were guaranteed a job somewhere you wanted to go. To get a job near home was an added bonus to the day's work.

One of the skills of driving a 'Sandy' was to quickly place the destination requested by the 'Billy Bunter'. Identify the area and establish north, south, east or west. If it's behind me, do a U-turn. If it's to the right, where's the first right hand turn and so on. Get the route in your brain, check it and get going. Then, if a single pin was in the back, open up a conversation. If it is a long trip, some drivers ask if there is a preferred route.

It paid to be polite to the cab fares. You only came back at them if they were rude or condescending, which usually happened at night when they were 'Brahms and Liszt'. It was quite common at night for visitors to London, from all parts north of the Watford gap and under the influence, to try to mimic a Cockney accent. I had my standard reply. "That's good, mate, at least on par with Dick Van Dyke in Mary Poppins." Everybody knew that Van Dyke's was the worst Cockney accent ever. 'Halliwell's Film Guide and Review' refers to "Mr Van Dyke's lamentable attempted Cockney." I couldn't understand why Tommy Steele, a singer and dancer with a strong London accent, never got the part. Who was the casting director? Van Dyke himself said they should have considered Ron Moody and that he was hampered by having an Irish speaker as voice coach.

Whenever I picked up a mum and daughter, looking for a decent tip, I always delivered the line, "Who's paying, you or your sister," to the mother. The mum would laugh and nine times out of ten, the daughter would smile, knowing I was giving her mum a compliment.

Other silliness was when they said, "Waterloo," and the reply would be, "The battle or the station?"

Back in the sixties there were around 6,500 licensed cab drivers and London was a good cab rider's manor. The only time I stopped was for a 'Nelson Riddle', which was a big problem in day work since the public 'Bengazis' were few and far between in central London. In Mayfair there was Hay's Mews. In Westminster, Horseferry Road, Storeys Gate and Ebury Bridge. Some hotels would let the cab drivers use their facilities. At night time you avoided Ebury Bridge toilet and eventually it was closed down because it had become a meeting place for men of a certain persuasion.

Hay's Mews also was closed but for a different reason. It was a top location in Mayfair, and the residents complained about the noise made by cabbies in the early hours, talking and closing cab doors.

I remember Hay's Mews with a bit of sadness. Over the years I seemed to bump into an elderly cab driver, never knowing his name, always at Hay's Mews. In conversation we always spoke about the previous day, good or bad. He told me he had been driving a cab for thirty years. Every night he gave all his money to his missus, and she gave him his two shillings six pence tea money, and made him his sandwiches to take to work. He told me he couldn't go home until he got the money his missus expected. He always looked poor, never seemed very happy, and told me he did long hours six days a week. Being the same size, I wanted to give him some of my clothes but didn't want to insult him. When Hay's Mews closed I only ever spied him in traffic and often wondered if his missus had made provision for him to retire or was it a case of old cab drivers never die, they just ride away!

At night, for me, it was important to make a female passenger travelling on her own feel comfortable. It's 1am and she's in the company of a complete stranger, so I always felt obliged to break the ice, rather than silence for fifteen or twenty minutes. Usually I would say "Old Kent Road, dear, which street? Okay, I know it, about fifteen minutes, no problems." I always would like the female members of my family to be treated the same way. When I got them to their destination, I always waited until they were safely inside.

There were anomalies from the Blue Book, expected routes compared to the actual routes taken because of traffic. The Blue Book expected you to go in the straightest line, so when plotting your route for the Knowledge you 'cottoned' the route on a map. I used pins, one at the start, one at the end with cotton thread tied around the two pins, giving the straightest line.

An example of a no-no is Paddington Station to Liverpool Street Station. The expected route was Bayswater Road into Oxford Street then on towards the City. Oxford Street has probably fifteen sets of traffic lights, plus pedestrian crossings. The popular way was Marylebone, Euston, Angel and down into the City. It was longer but much quicker, and few passengers ever complained.

Despite doing the Knowledge, there were always areas that were a bit cloudy. It didn't matter how many years I drove a cab I always had difficulty sorting out the Bedfords, which were all in the same vicinity: Bedford Avenue WC1; Bedford Place WC1; Bedford Row WC1; Bedford Square WC1; Bedford Way WC1; Bedford Street WC2; and Bedfordbury WC2.

There were various ways to obtain a vehicle to go to work. Today I advise the Knowledge boys in Edinburgh at the taxi school to give it six months before buying. That's what I did: learn the ropes on someone else's vehicle. There were various ways of hiring a cab. I went to the London General Cab Company which had a large fleet at the Oval. The options were:

1. A full flat cab seven days a week at £18 per week. Keep it and take it home.

2. 60/40 on the clock, whereby the owner kept 60% and the driver 40% plus tips and extras (e.g. passengers, cases and animals). The driver bought the diesel.

3. Half flat, change over 5pm from 5am at £9 per week.

Behind the desk was the cashier who dished out the cabs. I soon learned if I didn't give him his two and six, he would allocate me a dodgy cab. One in particular was driven by a guy called Smelly W--------- who wasn't used to 'Bob Hope' and the cab was 'Aunt Nelly'.

When I first got my cab badge I wrote off two cabs within the first four weeks. Neither accident was my fault.

One Sunday morning after the clubs had turned out I was in Cromwell Road heading towards Earls Court when an 'E' type Jag with a male driver and two females crossed into my lane and hit the cab head-on. The three of them were totally 'elephants'. The two girls sat on the kerb stunned, and the driver tried to make out it was down to me. I had passengers as witnesses as well as two other cab drivers. The police took the driver away.

Second time, I was waiting at the red light at the bottom of the Haymarket. As the lights changed I moved forward and saw an open-backed lorry overtaking me on a bend as I was going towards Trafalgar Square. I stopped and waited, as the back of the lorry took the front end of my cab away. Lucky for me, two policemen saw it all and were witnesses for me. The manager of the London General Cab Company, a gentleman called Jeffrey Trotter, called me into his office and accepted my story completely. He wasn't part of the Peckham Trotters; he was a very well educated public school boy and a man I later in life dealt with via the LTDA.

When I started driving a cab in the late sixties it was boom time for the tourist trade and the tourist season was great, from May to New Year. You rowed on all day long. At times when you dropped off one passenger, two more would try to claim the cab. You always took the one you saw first. Back then an average fare from Park Lane to Heathrow was three pounds seven shillings and sixpence. The flag fell at one shilling nine pence. The tank usually took £3 to £4 a day and takings were about £18 a day in winter and £28 a day in summer. In those days there was a Kipper Season from January to April. It was called Kipper because trade was flat and you to pick the bones out, that is, sort out where your work was.

Back when I started, a cab driver was not compelled to take a job over six miles, unless you wanted to quote a price that was acceptable to the fare. In my mind this was a big mistake. I always took everything as it came, never knowing what you might find on the way back. I believe the licensed trade played into the hands of the private hire. If jobs were taken regularly out to places like Tooting or Balham, the public would become used to seeing licensed cabs at the bottom of their road, instead of phoning the opposition.

Back when I started there was an unwritten code among London's licensed cab drivers. I have since learned that it also applied in Edinburgh, from Jim Kerlin and Bob McCulloch, both older drivers who teach at Jim's taxi school. If a driver had his light on looking for a job and he let an empty cab out of a side street (also plying for hire), the cab would wave the courteous driver in front to his original position, that is, first to pick up. Likewise, if the cab in front was empty and looking, you never overtook until he was hired. Perhaps this old code should be taught at the various knowledge schools, something I know my old pal Malcolm Linsky would welcome at his thriving training school in north London.

I learned a valuable lesson during my first Christmas driving a cab. There were always office parties, and inevitably there were people too drunk for public transport, so they looked for cabs. I was in the City of London and a lady in her fifties, probably a company secretary, stopped me and asked me to take a young lady out to Dagenham. Two women brought her out and put her on the back seat, giving me an address in deepest darkest West Ham country. The young lady went to sleep and when I got to the address she wouldn't wake up. I shouted, turned the lights on and off, with no luck. I knocked at the door of the address I had been given, but no reply.

Now, a cardinal rule is NEVER touch a female passenger to wake them up. So I find the local police station and ask for a WPC. I explained everything, and the WPC pulled and prodded until the young woman woke up. I took her back to the house and she paid me.

The lesson I learned was that in future I would only take a drunken woman home if she was accompanied by somebody attending the party. Which was a double-edged sword: firstly, there was no problem waking them up and secondly the other passenger either went back to the party or on somewhere else, making it a good job!

The London cab trade is amongst the more charitable groups anywhere to be found. There are numerous cab trade charities that have annual or biannual outings. The one I always attended was the Albany outing and once a year we went to Margate. The committee headed by Duke Dineen and George Owen arranged free diesel for the drivers. We all decorated our own cabs and the work day was given up to take our charges to the coast.

Our charges were all mentally handicapped or were deaf, and I always took the deaf children. The people of southeast London clapped as we went on our way with a police motor bike escort. Each cab had two passengers and a chaperone. If there was a boy and a girl in the back, there was a female minder and the male driver looked after the boy. On the outskirts of Margate we all lined up for the grand entrance. On one occasion the great Norman Wisdom came along the line of cabs and acted the fool as only he could do. What a great guy! The passengers and drivers loved him.

My deaf kids on the Albany Taxi outing – what characters, especially the little fella!

Over the years any celebrity appearing at Margate would do an act for the hundreds we took to the Winter Gardens for free. Norman Wisdom, Jim Davidson and Lulu, and many others all gave their time.

Food was provided but not before the rides. A cab driver and his wife had a group and everyone had a good old knees up. I'll never forget the faces of the cab drivers sitting in the passenger seats of the bumper cars while their charges drove them.

When the day was over we took our special guests home and received their parents' thanks. I went home and kissed my two kids while they were asleep and thanked God for their health.

When I look at the Queen's Honours List I think it should be made up of the taxi trades charity committees. Not only in London, as I know Liverpool, Edinburgh and Glasgow and numerous others do the same for the less privileged.

Back in the sixties it was a common thing for a cab driver to pick up a nurse in uniform late at night and not charge them. I personally never charged deaf people and loved the look on their faces when in sign language I refused the fare and had a chat with them. In all the years I drove, the deaf and blind travelled free as did the red-coated Chelsea Pensioners.

When I finally handed back my badge, I got a lovely letter from the Public Carriage Office. Over four decades I received two possible recommendations for coming to the assistance of the police in their line of duty. The first was back in the seventies, when a young police officer was being attacked on the corner of Leicester Square by two youths. Another cab driver and I jumped in to stop the attack and both youths ran away.

The second was a lot more dangerous.

I was plying for hire in Earl's Court Road around midnight, when a young policeman jumped in the back with his helmet in his hands. Out came the old cliché, "Follow that car!" The car in question was a Triumph sports car and had two punters in it.

I did my level best but they weren't slowing down, speeding through one-way Redcliffe Gardens, jumping the lights at Fulham Road near Chelsea Football Club. I was still on their 'Daily Mail' along the waterfront towards Battersea Bridge, but then they went the wrong side of the road, overtaking all in the correct lane. I was stuck behind several cars, my 'Sandy McNab' was only a couple of weeks old, and I had responsibilities to my family, so I gave it up. The PC was on his radio and got out looking a bit relieved. He took my details and thanked me.

I never knew the outcome of the chase or if I ever got the recommendations!

The very words associated with taxis as transport for hire, such as hackney or cab, are integral to the origin of the trade. Four-wheeled coaches for hire, called hackney carriages first appeared in London about 1625, and were so-named from the horses, French haquenées, which pulled them. The two-wheeled cabriolet de place was introduced from Paris in 1823, with cabriolet quickly shortened to 'cab'. Further improvements followed in the 1830, with a four-wheeled cab, drawn by a single horse, which could carry three passengers. The first mechanically driven taxicabs, powered by electricity, appeared in 1897, were followed by the more efficient petrol powered vehicles in 1904. By the year of the Great War began there were 8,397 taxis registered in London. The days of horse drawn carriages closed forever in 1947.

Such was the number and popularity of taxis in London that as early as 1906 the Metropolitan Police drew up a set of regulations for taxis, one of which is still in force today, which stipulates that taxis must have a turning circle of no more than twenty feet to cope with the narrow streets of London. So the London taxi, which grew in size over the course of the twentieth century until now it is a vehicle approximately twenty foot long and eight foot wide and still has the amazing twenty four foot turning circle.

The famous turning circle of the London taxi is down to the design of its rack and pinion in the steering box. Martin Harvey, cab driver, former cab fleet owner and a good friend of mine, describes how this comes in the form of a worm that rotates as the steering wheel is turned, to which a peg is connected to the groove in the worm. This section of the box is connected to a lower drop arm at the underside of the steering box that is locked in position to the main track rod.

You have three ball joints on the near-side passenger and three ball joints on the off-side driver's side. These are connected to near-side and off-side drag link arms that are locked into position on the inside of the front wheels that are attached to steel kingpins.

Any questions?

Transport for London
Public Carriage Office

Our reference: 303441

Mr R I Lewis
125D Clydesdale Road
Mossend
Bellshill
Lanarkshire
ML4 2QH

Public Carriage Office

15 Penton Street
London N1 9PU

Phone 0845 602 7000
Fax 020 7126 1897
www.tfl.gov.uk/pco

30 May 2008

Dear Mr Lewis,

I am writing to acknowledge receipt of your notification of retirement and to thank you for enclosing your original and copy taxi driver's licences and badge number 50715.

Now that you have decided to retire, I would like to take this opportunity to thank you for 39 years sterling service to the travelling public of London.

A review of your personal file reveals that during your years as a licensed taxi driver you have a record of which you can be justifiably proud. It is heartening to see that not one of your passengers felt the need to complain about your service or driving, which is a true indication of your commitment to your profession.

As a memento of your career, I am enclosing the first cab driver's licence issued to you in March 1969.

I trust that you will enjoy good health and happiness in your retirement.

Yours sincerely,

Mary Dowdye
Head of Standards and Regulations

MAYOR OF LONDON

A division of Transport for London
whose principal place of business is
Windsor House
42-50 Victoria Street
London SW1H 0TL

VAT number 756 2769 90

CHAPTER EIGHT
The Royals

It was a week before Christmas and I was parked at the top of Cadogan Lane, at the junction of Pont Street, Knightsbridge, waiting for a businessman who was in Agent Provocateur, a top lingerie shop, buying for his missus (so he said). A Daimler pulled up opposite the cab and out got the beautiful Princess Diana, closely followed by a burly bodyguard. She looked stunning and wore a checked costume with a fur collar. Our eyes met and I said "Merry Christmas to you and the boys." She was away from Charlie then.

"Thank you and the same to you and your family," she said, smiling radiantly.

"I don't expect to get a kiss for Christmas," I said tongue in cheek. She laughed and blushed.

The bodyguard gave me daggers and shook his head.

****

It was a winter's evening and I was in Charing Cross Road around the corner from Leicester Square where there was a film premier taking place. The traffic was at a standstill, one lane up, one lane down, with a gap in the middle of the road. A traffic policeman on a motorbike signalled for me to get over nearer the kerb. A royal car approached and in the back was Prince Charles en route to the film night. I was close enough to touch the window of his slow moving vehicle. Never one to be a shy wilting flower, I had my window down and said "Alright Charles?" and gave him the thumbs up. He smiled and gave me a royal nod.

****

One sunny afternoon I had two elderly American ladies in the back going to Victoria Station. They asked me, as we approached Buckingham Palace, if I had ever seen the Queen on my travels. "Yes, I see Her Majesty regularly," I said, lying through my teeth. Out of nowhere came a police motorbike rider, who signalled for me to stop to let a royal car out of a side turning. "There you go, ladies," I said pointing to the Queen, making out like it was a normal occurrence. The two ladies waved at Her Majesty and she raised her right hand to acknowledge them. I got a blinding tip and I expect the two ladies from Chicago dined out on that story for some time.

CHAPTER NINE
Cab Stories

The London cab trade throws up lots of contrasting personalities, all with their own opinions of life. Most taxi drivers are strong-minded. They stand up for what they believe. It's taken as given that there can never be unity or agreement on all topics. I got to know a lot of cab drivers young and old over the years, and we ate together between shifts with lots of stories, some tall and some amusing, all good camaraderie.

As you can imagine, we gave each other nicknames, for example:

Jamaican George; Lord Lucan; Gorgeous George; Long Day Lew; Farmer Wally; Boy King; Johnnie Blue Cab; Shotgun Eddie; Wine Waiter; Big Ears; Cincinnati Yid; Flash Eddie; Get 'Em in Bill; Brian the Iron; The Dog Catcher; The Grenadier Guard; The Overcoat; Soppy

Bollocks; Aussie Dave; Bobby Bookings; Chicken George; Colonel Comb-over; Rutland Gate Bob; Moby Dick; Two of Veg (Reg); Oats and Barley (Charlie); the Duke of Camberwell; The Scouser; Video Vic; Magnum (4'11" sitting tall) Moustache; Eddie Calvert; Soapy Bob; Captain Birdseye; the Snide Yank; Phil the Spanner Thrower; and the Camper.

There's a popular saying "the day they issued the second badge, the cab trade was divided". The following is a compendium of the best stories and anecdotes from my time as a London cab driver. Make of it what it you will. It was great times and great people. You won't see their like again.

****

Cab Drivin' Characters

Aussie Dave

There were always plenty of 'wind-up merchants' in the cab trade and no one was better than Aussie Dave, who had been on 'the Knowledge' at the same time as me. He got his nickname because he recently had returned from Down Under.

One sunny morning, I am sitting at the lights in Piccadilly, looking at Eros, with two young ladies in the back of the cab. Before the lights went green, another cab pulled alongside mine with Aussie Dave in the driver's seat. He tapped on the passenger's window and in a camp voice, pointing at me, he said, "He broke my heart. We lived together and then he ran away with a young black man. I still love him and want him back."

Out of the corner of my mouth I said a two-word profanity and was never more pleased to see the lights turn green!

Ray Garcia's 'New Barnet Fair' (Hair)

Thirty-five years before Wayne Rooney thought about it, or was even born, Ray Garcia had the hair transplant. The hair was taken from the back of his neck and placed in a pattern in the front, in what looked like black peas. Being a London cab driver, you needed to be thick skinned if you went into a cafe or shelter where other cab men ate. Taking the 'pee' was rife. We all heard he had spent a fortune and were eagerly waiting to see Ray.

He came into the cafe and nobody laughed. I said, "Hello, Raymondo. Where did you get the barnet done? In Wigmore Street?"

"No," he said, not realising the wig bit.

"Was it in *Air* Street?"

"No," he said, still not sussing the puns with his barnet and London streets. Nobody laughed outwardly.

Later that day the dispatcher on the work radio was trying to cover a job in New Barnet, "Come on gents, who wants New Barnet?"

About six of us hit the button and said, "Tango 19 (Ray's call sign). I want New Barnet."

The radio circuit erupted.

As a footnote, Ray's transplant was a success in the front but he was bald at the back.

Lord Lucan

Another 'pee' take was when one of our number who looked remarkably like Lord Lucan – eyebrows met, snobby aristocratic look, piggy eyes – parted and dyed his hair and became a real lookalike. He had dyed his hair blond, which, if he were the real lord, could have been part of the disguise.

He was greeted by, "Are you dying to tell us something?"

Someone slipped outside to a phone box to tell 999 that Lucky Lucan was in a cafe in Waterloo Road. The police turned up and saw the likeness and after cab licence was produced, they laughed and went away. The Lucan lookalike pointed several fingers but never found out 'who dunnit'.

Later in life I read a good book that convinced me that Lord Lucan died penniless in Goa.

JBC – Johnnie Blue Cab

Like most people, I have my own pet hates: women wearing black tights and trainers; a greeting of "Hello, you" said in a twee way; fake kissing of both cheeks with the sound of 'mwahh'; and older men wearing Yankee baseball caps.

So, I'm in traffic outside Harrods when in amongst the buses, cars and cabs I spy JBC sporting a New York baseball cap, set at a rakish angle on his head. Later, in the restaurant at Waterloo with all the boys, I casually said, "You know what really winds me up?"

"What?" a mouthful of food replied.

"Why would an older London cab driver with no allegiance to New York wear a baseball cap? It really looks naff." All round the table nodded and grunted between mouthfuls.

JBC said, "You're right. I think they are trying to recapture their youth."

When we left the cafe, I put a cigar in my mouth and walked towards JBC's cab.

"Got a light, John?"

He opened his cab door to get his matches and there on the floor in the luggage side was the offending article. To myself I said, "Gotcha", and smiled.

The cap was never seen again. I loved JBC and had to be subtle.

Columbia 100–1 Outsiders

During a World Cup, one of our many football pundits said, "Put your house on Columbia to win it." The entire table laughed.

After Columbia's early exit from the Cup, I walked into the cafe with an empty suitcase but gave the impression it was heavy.

The pundit said, "What's he got that f...ing suitcase for?"

"What have I got the suitcase for? Last time I fucking listen to you. I'm homeless."

East Meets West

There was guy who did the Knowledge the same time as me and was an expert on boxing: in what round, at what venue, how many fights etc. etc. He was a good-looking guy who in his younger days looked like Bobby Moore.

He met a lady who was very much a Sloane Ranger who fell for his good looks and rough diamond, Cockney manners. It got serious, and she wanted mummy and daddy to meet him, have a meal together.

They booked a table in a top Italian restaurant in South Kensington, and all was going well until the prospective father-in-law asked the would-be son-in-law to choose the wine. Now, ask him to order a fry-up or a pie and mash, no problems. But wine in a POSH joint, no way. He looked at the wine list and ordered a bottle of 'Bow Jollis'.

Shortly afterwards, the romance ended but the wind up in the cafe lasted for years with him being nicknamed the 'Wine Waiter'.

The Boy King

One of the drivers was the opposite of your typical London cab driver: he only spoke if necessary and wasn't very endearing. You could get more conversation from Harpo Marx. On this occasion he sat outside the Dorcester Hotel, first on the rank outside, when out came a large American gentleman who, in a Southern accent, said, "Tootin' Cahmen."

About thirty minutes later the driver asked the punter whereabouts do you want, to which he replied, "The Exhibition."

The driver was six miles deep in south-west London in Tooting Common. His nickname thereafter was 'the Boy King' or 'the Mummy.'

Hugh Grant

He came into the cafe looking very smug. We all knew his reputation for tall stories but this time he had us all.

"All right? You're looking happy."

"Had a great day yesterday. Put in on the Hilton rank about 8am; two Japs came out and asked to go to Reading. I get there, ask a local cab where the trading estate is, find it no trouble. They ask me to wait and take 'em back to London. I drop them in Regents Street. As far as I'm concerned, end of.

In the afternoon I'm on the Hilton again and déjà vu: the two 'brandy snaps' come out again. When they recognise me they are deliriously happy, saying 'Go back Reading.' Same again: wait and back to the Hilton.

By now it's about time I made tracks home. I'm in Camden Town when an old lady wants to go to Chingford Cemetery. Drop her off, turn off the 'hickory' and go home. I walk in and the missus asks, "What kind of day did you have?"

"Four Readings and a funeral."

****

Stories from the Frontline

The Witty Dispatcher

Before the days of the sophisticated computerised radio work channels, it was all voice. You hit your button and gave a position for the job being called and the dispatcher was God: he adjudicated who was the best cab.

This system produced some funny guys and some 'little Hitlers'. When you listen to the same patter for hours on end it can be tedious. However, there was one dispatcher who was great value with his wit, as per two examples below.

"Hello 56. I'd open the window if I was you."

"No," I said. "I just started."

"Oh, I thought you said you just farted!"

Or

"Where are you, 21?"

"Outside Madame Tussauds."

"Don't hang about, they're stock taking!"

No matter what he said, the whole radio circuit could only hear him, so if you took exception – tough.

And if you lost your temper, you were put on complaint. Being on complaint meant that a committee of fellow cab drivers decided your fate – a one week or two week suspension, for example. My big pal Barry Addinall thought his complaint was a load of crap so he replied on toilet paper to the letter informing him of the charge and was banned sine die. No sense of humour!

George the Scouser

Back in the early seventies there was a story in the 'News of the World' about a Liverpool seaman called George

Jamieson who had a sex change and became April Ashley. There was a before and after picture of him in the paper. So I'm driving down the King's Road, Chelsea about 3am Sunday morning when the clubs chucked out, and there with her hand up, dressed in black, was a butch-looking woman.

"Ladbroke Gardens, driver," said in a deep voice.

All the way there 'she' was chatting me up, sitting on the pull-down seat. I was playing along.

When we arrive 'she' says, "Would you like to come up, driver?"

"No thanks, George."

"You bastard," he hissed in a camp manner.

George recently received a gong from the Queen for being the first to have the operation. Can you believe that? He got an award for having his three-piece suite taken away - hardly Victoria Cross criteria for bravery. Or is it?

Syrup of Fig

I was sitting on Sloane Square rank on windy morning when a very posh lady approached the cab and asked to go to Harrods. We engaged in conversation and she said, "Very windy today, driver."

"I know, love, my 'syrup of fig' has been off twice."

I looked in the mirror and saw her looking for a join in my hair (incidentally all my own) and she said sadly, "I know the problem. My husband wears one."

Straight on, Driver

I liked to go to work looking tidy and at the time Lacoste cardigans were very popular. I had a yellow one with my initials, R.L., on my left chest.

I'm in Harley Street and a dizzy blonde gets in the cab. We talk and she says, "What does R.L. on your cardigan mean?"

"Well," I said, "I'm not good at directions, so if you say turn left driver, I look down to see which way I should go."

"What a good idea, driver."

MOTD

I was a brand new cab driver and it was a wintery Saturday night, 9.15pm, and I was near Arsenal's ground. A scruffy man about forty years of age asked me to take him to

Dalston Junction. He told me his wife had left him and he was going to get her back at his mother-in-law's house. He directed me round some back streets until we can to an estate of prefabs. He told me to wait, he wouldn't be ten minutes, and then back to Highbury.

It was a freezing night. I lit a cigar, pulled the window down, and heard an almighty row going on. Things went quiet and then another row. This went on for about five minutes and then I realised I had a runner. The next thing I heard was 'Da da da da da da da' and Jimmy Hill's voice. I was listening to BBC One and Match of the Day. After this lesson I was always more cautious with "I'll be back in five minutes." Another time an Irishman got out of the cab in Lisson Grove and said he would go up to his flat and get the money. "Okay, leave your 'nanny goat'". He obliged. Thirty minutes later, no show. Lesson learned – no payment but my Dad had a few good years out of it after dry cleaning.

Mrs Sir Alex Ferguson

I was on point at Harrods when a lady came out, carrying a hat box and wanted to go to Euston Station. I was living in Scotland at the time and the lady was Scottish. We struck up a conversation and she told me she had bought a hat for her son's forthcoming wedding. I asked her what part of Scotland she lived in and she replied that she lived in Cheshire. Looking at her closely in the mirror, I asked her if she was Mrs Alex Ferguson, which she confirmed, adding, "All you London cab drivers are know-alls."

While I recognise Sir Alex to be one of, or possibly the greatest, football managers of all time, I can never forgive him for his lack of people skills. In an article written by Sarah Getty in 'The Metro', she quotes Sir Alex as stating, "Beckham's a Londoner. He's a bit flash at times. I think it's the make-up of London people, to be honest." Unquote.

While I agree that I am, and numerous other Londoners known to me, could be called 'pie and mash', I find it very dangerous to generalise to the extent of saying, "It's the make-up of London people." My Dad and uncles were certainly not flash, and it would be unkind of me to say, "All people from Govan have red noses and don't have any people skills." Very dangerous to generalise, Sir Alex!

Did You Say Missionary?

It was 3am. I was almost home, when two gay young men stopped me and simply said, "Crouch End," which was at least twelve miles away in the opposite direction. Never one to mind my words I said, "Is that where you live or is it a position?" They laughed and I took them to their destination.

Runners

There are two stories about runners, both with happy endings.

I was in Paddington about 2am when a large Teddy boy, complete with a Tony Curtis haircut, asked to go to Newington Green, which was a good ride about five miles away. When we got there, he leans in the window asking, "How much?"

Before I can answer he has it away on his toes, but it was all in slow motion as his size stops him from being a sprinter. He was a big man, possibly twenty stone, completely out of breath. I am driving along side of him saying, "Turn it in, mate." He crossed the road; I did a U-turn. In the end he just gave up, lent on the window gagging for air, and paid me.

It was snowing and an old pal dropped a job off in Ridley Road Market around midnight. Usual banter of "How much?" to disarm you and then they take off. My pal, being on the heavy side, was slow out of the blocks and the sprinter had a ten yard start. Thankfully, because of the icy conditions, the runner takes a tumble. My friend now has his foot on the prostrate man's throat. "Pay up," my mate says, pressing harder on the man's chest with his heel. The punter struggles through his pockets and produces a £20 note, which my mate pockets and gets back in his cab.

"What about my change?" the man asks. "Behave yourself," my mate says, driving off. All because of a £5 fare he had more than enough to pay for!

Tips

Tommy Cooper was a cab user and lived in Chiswick, west London, and always paid his fare with "have a drink on me", putting a 'tea bag' in your 'German Band'.

I know this is generalising, but the worst tippers were the Australians, closely followed by the French. I once asked an Aussie why they never tipped, and he gave a logical answer: "Our unions expect our living wage to be good enough not to need tips."

The best without a doubt were Londoners; you could work working class areas on a Friday and Saturday night and take home good money. A guy gets in your cab with his missus or partner, "Red Lion, pal", six shillings on the clock, puts a 'cow' through the window with a "Keep it."

After the Cockneys came the Yanks and the Japanese.

Being in a job where tips are expected when a good service is given, e.g. get me to the airport in thirty minutes "can you pick up my mum at this address and take her to…"

I always tip in restaurants 10% to 15%, depending on service especially where young kids are working their way through college.

So compare the working class, (which I suspect is the same in Liverpool, Manchester, Glasgow and Edinburgh) to the Belgravia mob. It was always the same: "take a bob" – a shilling. These people obviously teach their kids at an early age to "give the taxi man a shilling". To highlight this, I was at Paddington Station and a young boy with his trunk was coming home from Eton for the holidays. I loaded the trunk, and he wanted Chester Square, Belgravia. Very politely, he paid me and said, "Take a bob for yourself, driver."

The best tip I ever had was on my Dad's seventieth birthday. On the previous Saturday, we had a party for him and all his pals and family were there. I was in Knightsbridge and an Indonesian gent got in for the Hilton Park Lane. Not much of a job, but we chatted, and he gave me a £2 tip.

The next fare went to Paddington Station and handed me a leather bag shaped like a rugby ball through the window. I pulled round at the back of the station and opened the bag to see what was in the bag to see who it belonged to. Inside were passport, car keys, American dollars, foreign currency and credit cards: in short, everything a travelling man needed. I looked at the passport and its owner was Mr Lee, the Indonesian gent.

So I pulled up at the Hilton with the bag and asked the doorman if anybody had missed anything. He said he would take the bag and find Mr Lee – I don't think so.

I walked into the foyer of the Hilton and Mr Lee was at the desk trying to book in without his passport. He saw me and said, "I knew you would come back!" He cuddled me, turned his back on me, took his bag and placed notes in my hand. I thanked him and didn't count the notes until I was outside: *four* £50 notes.

The Publicans

I was working at Wimbledon Village in the early hours, hoping for a job that would take me somewhere near home. A hand went up. It was a 'him and her', and my prayers were answered: the job was a pub I knew about two miles from home.

About fifty years old, he had a suit, collar and tie, balding and glasses, a bit like Reg from the supermarket on 'Coronation Street'. She was in her mid-forties, dolled up to the nines as you expect the publican's wife to be when out on the town.

It was about a six mile fare. At first, all was quiet; they were sitting at opposite ends of the back seat.

Then, it started.

It was obviously their second time around at the marriage game: "As for your son, he just a waster!"

"Your daughter has had her last penny from me!" etc. etc.

She said, "Fuck you!" and threw a right-hand with his glasses at an angle and he went down on his knees. His head, dripping blood from a cut over his eye with his glasses at an angle, appeared at the connecting window. "Carry on, driver," he said.

I stopped the cab and told them to behave themselves or out! No more was said. I saw her give him a handkerchief to wipe the blood away.

We get to the pub and she looks into my window and says, "Thank you, driver. Goodnight" and sashays away as if butter wouldn't melt in her mouth. He tells me to take £3 for a tip and puts his hand in the passenger window to shake hands with me. "Goodnight, driver. All the best."

For them just a normal night out.

The Ten-Yard Test
Back in the early seventies, the labourers came over from Ireland for work in London. Their best 'bib and tucker' was the double-breasted 'whistle and flute' with wide trousers and turn-ups, and, after the 'rubber dubs' chucking out time they were looking for us in Cricklewood, Camden and County Kilburn.

We saw the suits that were definitely not Saville Row style and, knowing their penchant for Guinness, we doubted their being sober at 1am. So we did the ten yard test: pull up ten yards past the would-be fare and if he walked straight, no problem. If he swayed, it was good night nurse.

All this was great until the fashion became wide-lapel, double-breasted suits with 'Lionel Blairs', and we were not at the races in spotting the bhoyo.

On the subject of the sons of the Emerald Isle, one night I was in Edgware Road stuck in traffic with my light out on the way home. Seamus staggered towards the cab and tried to get in. My doors were locked for the night.

"I'm going to Cricklewood."

"Sorry, mate, I'm finished for the night."

"*You bastard!* I'll fight you!"

"Ok," I said, "Go round the corner."

He went round, taking his coat off in readiness. The traffic moved and I waved, saying, "Good night and God bless!"

Murder

One Saturday evening about 8pm I was driving along Old Park Lane when out of a 'battle cruiser' ran a wild looking man in his thirties, with long black hair and a beard.

"Vauxhall Bridge," he panted.

As we went along he chatted and I noticed blood on his shirt. He asked me if I was "one of our own" which meant, in short, a Cockney with all the principles that implies: no grassing and looking after your own before the police.

When we got to Vauxhall he asked me to take him on further to Camberwell. He paid me well and asked me not tell anyone where I dropped him.

On the front page of Monday's papers was the headline "Man Killed in Park Lane Pub" and the police wanted witnesses. The story was a man was struck over the head with a soda siphon in the pub and died.

On Monday night, I sat at home looking into the dark garden, thinking. I thought of my responsibilities and my wife and two children asleep upstairs, a court case that would put me in the limelight with possible reprisals, or of doing the right thing and go forward as a witness.

My problem was solved by the first editions on Tuesday: somebody in the pub knew the killer and he was arrested.

The Queen of England
It was the sixties and my second Saturday night in the cab, early morning spilling into Sunday. I was in Wood Lane, Shepherds Bush, which wasn't my best manor for knowledge.

He put his hand up and in a drunken slur he said, "Do you know the Queen of England?"

Being tired and thinking he was just a babbling drunk, I said, "Yeah, mate, where do you want to go?"

He repeated, "Do you know the Queen of England?"

I lost a bit of patience and drove away.

Two weeks later I was in Goldhawk Road, Shepherds Bush, and in the middle of the road at a junction was a pub called – you guessed it.

The Skiver

One Sunday I was at Victoria Station and a young man got in for Peckham Rye. We were talking when we were going over Vauxhall Bridge but he had disappeared. I looked round and saw him lying on the floor.

"Keep driving, mate," he said. "My guvnor is in the next car next to us and I've been off sick for the last two weeks!"

Worst Night Ever

It was a Friday night about 8.30pm and I picked up in Westbourne Park Road. The job was a 'him and her' and she was 'elephants'. They wanted to go to Cricklewood.

They got out, paid the exact fare and walked away. I always look round to see if anything was left in the back and yes, there is: a pool of water where she had sat. I dried it up the best I could, but the seats were velour, not leather.

The next two were fully fledged punks, Johnnie Rotten lookalikes, and they wanted to go to some dodgy council estate in Burnt Oak. They told me to stop. I asked for the fare through the window because I fancied they would do a runner. This proved to be the case: they reached for the door handle but couldn't get out as all the time my foot was on the 'Hattie's'. So, after much arguing and swearing and threats, they paid up, and slunk away.

The night was to get worse.

I drove down the road want to get back to the centre of town and civilisation.

At a bus stop there were two Irishmen, one a giant in an oversized raincoat and the other my build about five foot eight and barrel-chested.

"The Cock," was all he said. I knew it was a pub in Cricklewood with a large forecourt. It was one straight road from the bus stop to the pub. At The Cock, the back door opened and the Giant slowly walked away, leaving the miniature Victor McLagen snarling, "You came the long way. If want your money you will have to fight me."

By now, with the two previous jobs, I had the hump and badly wanted Paddy to release my anger. A cab driver I knew slightly was on the forecourt, waiting to see what was going to happen. Paddy shaped up and I kicked him up 'the Niagras' but, to give him his due, he kept coming forward. We finished up against the cab, punching each other.

Out of the blue, a police van pulled in and a Glaswegian sergeant growled, "Pay the man!"

Paddy argued that I went the long way and after listening, my friend the sergeant repeated, "Pay the man."

The sergeant said, "How much do you want, Cabbie?" I looked at the clock and saw £5. Paddy went berserk, "It was only £3 when I got out."

I said, "Ah, but we've just had three times three-minute rounds."

I got the £5, thanked the sergeant and pulled into the main road. A little girl, about seventeen years old, stopped me and asked to go to Harrow Road. When I got to her flat, she said she had to go up to her parents to get the fare. By now I'd had enough and said, "Darling, have it down to me."

It was a bad night and it wasn't about to get better. So I decided to go home early and see if I could catch the wife with the milkman.

Rorke's Drift

One Saturday afternoon I took an elderly black lady to Brixton. She had two large suitcases that I loaded in the cab for her. When we got to our destination, she paid me and asked me to carry the cases to the bottom of a multi-story block of flats. The cab was stopped in a street with cars parked on both sides of the road and was blocking traffic in both directions. I apologised to the black lady driver of the Volvo stopped behind my cab and gestured to stop to the approaching vehicle whilst I took the cases to the lift for the elderly woman. All part of the service or so I thought.

When I came back to the cab, the approaching vehicle, a two-door BMW, had gone nose to nose with my cab. Stalemate. No one could move.

In the BMW was the driver – a Lionel Ritchie lookalike – and a Rasta in the passenger seat smoking pot and in the back a double for Mike Tyson in a tracksuit and patterned haircut.

I said to Lionel Ritchie, "I did ask you to wait, mate. Now we've got a traffic jam."

His reply was a seven-letter word that begins with 'b' and ends in 's', a word that in rhyming slang means 'orchestral stalls'.

I got back in my cab and sat there. The woman in the Volvo was out spitting feathers, "Now look what you've done!"

"I was only helping an elderly lady with cases, as you could see."

She thought about it and said to Lionel Ritchie, "You need to reverse."

After a few choice words he complied with her request. By now a small crowd had gathered on the pavement, mainly young kids looking to see if any excitement was about to occur. They weren't disappointed.

As Lionel reversed to the spot where I could get through, he spat at me, catching me full in the face. Despite feeling like Michael Caine at Rorke's Drift, I lost the plot. I threw a right-hander through his open window, drawing blood.

The Rasta didn't move but the young Tyson couldn't get out past the two in front.

Was I ever pleased.

Lionel got a yellow crook-lock from the floor and tried to get out of the car. In my rage I slammed the door on his legs and went back to the cab to find something to defend myself with. On the floor of the cab was a wooden brush no more than eight inches long. I threw the brush, which missed Lionel, and went through the BMW's back screen, and cartoonlike, the brush shape held until all the glass shattered. Discretion being the better part of valour, I had the cab away, not stopping until I got to Camberwell Green a couple of miles away.

Am I home scot-free? No, I'm not.

A couple of weeks later, I got a phone call from PC Robson at Brixton Police Station. He informed me that was on ABH, criminal damage and road rage charges. Furthermore, I was to attend Brixton nick the next day.

The woman in the Volvo had taken my number and given it to the police and they traced me at the Public Carriage Office.

The next day I walked into Brixton Police Station and asked for PC Robson. He took me to an interview room where an Inspector joined us. I explained what had happened and didn't leave anything out. At the end of my tale, I said to the young PC, "What would you have done if it was your face with spit all over it?"

The Inspector interrupted and told his colleague not to answer.

The Inspector told me that Lionel was a drug addict and had been on the phone being abusive to his officers, and all he wanted was my name and address, and payment for the shattered back screen of his car. None of my particulars were given out, and eventually common sense prevailed: none of the charges were taken further.

Fourteen years later, I am still adamant I was only doing my job by helping an OAP. I didn't choose to spit in anyone's face, and if I had, I would have expected retribution. None of this episode or any others was recorded on my cab driver's broadsheet.

The Opposition

The animosity between the licensed trade and the private hire or mini cabs was fearsome. In the early days, their vehicles were blocked in when trying to nick our work, and some were severely damaged. The thinking was, we do our apprenticeship on the knowledge of London with no pay. They get a car with no knowledge and go into competition for work, receiving cash from the word go. The sad thing was, that some mini cab drivers considered themselves to be the same as us, bona fide licensed trade cab drivers.

So, when they came alongside in traffic with us, the punters in the back asking directions, they were faced with standard replies.

"How do I get to the Albert Hall?"

"Practice the violin."

"How do I get to the Old Bailey?"

"Do a bank job."

"How do I get to Euston Station?"

"Best by Underground."

"What's the quickest way to Kilburn?"

"Are you driving?"

"Yes."

"That's the quickest way."

No Smoking Day

In the sixties, front-page news was that an East End gangster and a Lord had been co-habiting. Questions were raised in Parliament. I believe this contributed, apart from gangland activities, to the thirty-year stretch meted out to Ronnie Kray, because of his connections in high places. Photos showed Lord Boothby, Ronnie Kray and Leslie Holt (another East End rascal) all enjoying each other's company.

This is all background to the following.

I picked up a lady clad in a cheap fur coat in Marylebone High Street who asked to go Carlton Towers Hotel. Her cheap fur shed itself all over my velour backseat. Completely unaware that it was No Smoking Day, I pulled into the hotel forecourt with a cigar on. There was a job, in a beautiful dark cashmere overcoat, waiting and smoking a cigarette. He asked the doorman for me because I was smoking and he knew what day it was. He smoked all the way to the House of Lords. When he got out, the back of his overcoat was covered in bits of cheap fur left by the previous passenger. He paid me and a policeman at the door called out, "Lord _____, your backside has fur on it."

He looked at me and I said, "Don't think for one minute

I'm going to interfere with your backside after the last turn out with a Lord and a commoner. He laughed, and as quick as a flash he said, "Oh, yes, Boothby and that Kray chappie."

Poor Diction

After sitting in the Dorcester for ten minutes, I was on point (i.e. first) in the taxi rank. A toff came out and said, "Pembridge Square."

In reply, I said, "Notting Hill Gate?" by way of confirming the area and he walked away.

I called him back, asking what was wrong and he said, "I thought you said not in here mate."

Dennis Nilsen (Probably)

About 1am I was in Shaftebury Avenue when a bespeckled man, with a youngster about seventeen years old, hailed my cab. He asked for Cranley Gardens, and knowing there were two, I asked which one, hoping it was the one in Earls Court.

"No," he said, "Muswell Hill."

Disappointed to be going about twenty miles away from home, I put on the 'hickory' and lit a cigar. When I looked in the back, I saw the two punters cuddling into one another. I wasn't pleased, but nothing too outrageous. When we arrived at Cranley Gardens, Binsy legals me off: exact fare, no tip. I turned the cab around and headed back to the centre for work.

Some years later, I read in the 'linen draper' of a murderer who lived in Cranley Gardens, Muswell Hill, and who preyed on rent boys. Dennis Nilsen was his name.

Nilsen confessed to fifteen murders and was a real sicko. He sketched his victims, strangled them with a tie, and preserved their bodies for days before chopping them up. The outside drains became blocked and a plumber found human remains, including a finger. So it was good night nurse for Dennis and long overdue for the missing boys' families.

Six Into Four Don't Go

It was 2am and I was sitting at a red light in Commercial Road in the East End. Two buildings blocked any view, either left or right around the pavement and around the corner. Suddenly, six black youths, all very well dressed, ran around the corner and opened the passenger doors.

"Hold up fellas. I am only licensed for four passengers," I said, trying to reason with them. By now, all six are in the cab, and I am feeling a bit uncomfortable.

"Just fucking drive to London Fields," a voice said from the back.

London Fields is an open space and I am imagining my fate.

As I approached Bethnal Green Road, I intended to aim for the police station and seek sanctuary, leaving the punters in the back, but a voice said, "Where you going? Turn left here." Obviously local boys.

I get to London Fields; two get out.

"Shacklewell Lane." I was ordered.

Two more get out.

"Stamford Hill," a final request came through the glass.

My thoughts by this time were that if they run, which was commonplace with young riders in the wee hours, I am going to wipe my mouth with the lost fare and go home.

"Pull up here. How much do you want?" Music to my ears.

I had taken a liberty and clocked up all the extras for five (first in goes free), and received the exact fare, no tip, and was delighted that they paid me. I think that fare gave me a few grey hairs!

That's The One My Brother Knows

Although my cab driving days are over, I still get phone calls from family asking where such and such street is in the City or in the West End. Despite my failing memory, after a couple of minutes I can come up with the goods. Whenever I'm watching 'The Apprentice' and the arrival shot of the East End and the City of London, I say to myself "I knew 95% of all those streets." But more to the point, it reminds me of a great story.

Some years ago, a London cab driver was on a radio programme where he boasted that between him and his brother they knew every single street in London. As the programme unfolded, the driver answered several questions and he was impressing all concerned. When they threw one that had him stumped, the wag replied, "Ah, that's one my brother knows!"

Wanna Phone a Friend?

At the height of 'Who Wants to be A Millionaire'. I was sitting on the rank at Liverpool Street Station, when a man in his fifties came up to the cab. "Where to, mate?" I enquired. He was completely speechless and couldn't remember his destination. I gave him a couple of minutes but he still couldn't remember. Keeping a straight face I said, "Do you want to phone a friend?" He laughed and remembered.

Celebrities (and Me)

In Dick Whittington's time London's streets were paved with gold. Over the years the streets have become paved with celebrities. And yes, I have to say it is one of the perks of the trade that cabbies get more opportunity than most to meet, so to speak, the celebs of the day. Whenever a celeb got into the cab alone he or she is fair game for a conversation. However, if they had fellow travellers I never interrupted their privacy unless they spoke first. Here's the best.

Charlie Watts

Charlie Watts is probably the joint most famous rock n roll drummer, along with Ringo Starr. He is also a good guy.

In December 1971 my daughter Alex was born and I'd a few days off, anxiously pounding the waiting room at St Thomas's, Waterloo, On my first day back to work, a hand went up in Mayfair to go to the King's Road. After checking the mirror, I saw it was Charlie Watts, well dressed as usual. He asked if I was busy and I explained I was just back after the birth of my Alex. He asked when and told me his daughter was born the same day; I think he said her name was Seraphina but it's forty years ago to be too sure. Anyway, we had a good chat and he gave me a £2 tip, which was a good tip back then, and then gave me a 'Lady Godiva' to put in Alex's savings.

From working class stock – one of my own.

Anthony Newley

I was listening to BBC radio in the cab. It was Anthony Newley's sixty fifth birthday and he was in London. The next day, a suave guy in a red cashmere jumper accompanied by a beautiful blonde, probably in her fifties, stopped me in Portland Place and wanted to go to Channel Four TV.

I said, "Tony, why do want a cab, now you've got your bus pass?"

He laughed and said to the blonde, "Only in London, cheeky bleeder."

Anthony Newley was an East End boy who did well for himself, first as the Artful Dodger in the 1948 version of 'Oliver Twist' and later on Broadway. He made over fifty films in Hollywood and married Joan Collins.

We had a conversation about the East End and where he had lived. He was a gentleman. He paid me well and we shook hands. He looked fit, handsome and suave.

A short time later, he was taken seriously ill and passed away.

The American Prince

I was driving through Chester Square, Belgravia and spied Bernie Swartz aka Tony Curtis pushing a buggy with his son in it. Being brought up on 'Yonder is de castle of my fodder', I couldn't resist a chat with a Hollywood legend. What a great guy! We talked for about ten minutes about his films, life and family. I got the impression he was lonely and only too pleased to talk.

The conversation stopped when an old dowager saw my cab – the 'for hire' sign was on – and she wanted Harrods. We shook hands and I will never forget 'The American Prince' as he called his autobiography.

One of the Goons

Down the Fulham Road was a top Indian Restaurant and the doorman, dressed in the full Monty complete with turban, stopped me to do a delivery for which I had to pay up front and get the money back from the punter who ordered it. When I saw the name of this punter, I didn't argue about paying.

I was instructed to go to an address in Mayfair and press the bell for the penthouse.

"Come up, driver," the voice said.

I stepped out of the lift and into a penthouse that I'd only ever seen the likes of on the silver screen. There was a lady sitting on a large sofa in a kaftan who said hello.

"How much do I owe you altogether, fare and meal?" he asked.

I told him and he gave me an extra £5 and patted me on the back.

I said, "Enjoy your 'ruby' and good night." It was Inspector Clouseau – Peter Sellers.

Tom Selleck

On a sunny morning in Pall Mall, Magnum stopped me. He wanted the Berkeley Hotel in Knightsbridge. He was at least six foot four and was sporting his trademark 'Bon Marche'. I told him my favourite film of his was 'An Innocent Man' that was made in 1989 with F. Murray Abrams. He was very pleased. When we got to the hotel, at the front of the taxi rank was Johnny Blue Cab or JBC, who spied me with Tom Selleck.

Magnum paid me well and was up the stairs of the front entrance, when I heard "Tom, Tom". It was JBC trying to get Selleck's attention. Did he ever pay for that! When JBC walked into the Waterloo cafe that evening about eight drivers shouted out "Tom, Tom!"

Jeanne Moreau

One Sunday afternoon I was ranked outside the Westbury, off Bond Street. The luggage came out and I thought, "I've cracked it here; it's an airport." Out came Jeanne Moreau, a French actress I grew up with when my Dad took me to the French cinemas. Since 1948 she had appeared in French classics, notably among them 'Jules and Jim' in 1961 and later on in Hollywood. She made over a hundred films.

She wanted a hotel in Knightsbridge and we chatted. I told her I was reading a book called 'Schindler's Ark', and she showed interest. I only had a few pages left to finish and I told her I would leave the book for her at her hotel. She thanked me and tipped well. The next day I called at the hotel to check if she was still there; she was and the receptionist took the book for her. End of story, except I told all the boys later in life that Jeanne Moreau had given the book to Steven Spielberg who made 'Schindler's List' based on it. Who knows?

George Best and a Scottish Football Legend

A regular cab user in London was George Best, a very convivial man, who was always 'Brahms and Liszt'. He always said three words, "Take me home" and all the cab drivers knew he lived in Phene Street, Chelsea, next to the pub. He was a good tipper and never a problem. One night he came out of a club with a well known film star and asked to go to a trendy address in north London. After about five minutes into the journey, I moved my mirror down to avert my eyes from the goings on in the back seat. When we arrived at the lady's address, she got out and kissed him good night. True to form, George said the normal three words, "Take me home."

Another northern footballer, who shall remain nameless, wasn't so lucky sexually when he came out of a club a bit worse for wear with a blonde in tow. An acquaintance of mine said, as they were going along past the Albert Hall, there was shouting and swearing from the back of the cab before the blonde was summarily ejected out of the cab. It turned out that the 'woman' wasn't a woman at all, but a guy in drag.

Johnnie Vaughan

I was about to go to the toilet in Horseferry Road when Johnnie Vaughan asked if I was for hire. I told him to get in the cab while I had a quick 'Nelson Riddle'. I came out and he said, "Fulham". He asked what team I supported and when I said Millwall, he laughed and told me he was a Chelsea man.

We got talking about films, which as a film buff suited me. He really surprised me with his knowledge of old films and went into a soliloquy from 'Bad Day at Black Rock' as done by Spencer Tracey in the film. Not to be out done, I did the classic 'On the Waterfront' scene set in the back of the cab between Brando and Steiger. Then I gave him a few movie questions and he to me. It was a good fare. He said, "You are different to most cabbies; they want to talk about football, but I love the movies. If you were younger, I'd knock about with you as a pal, but unfortunately you are too old."

Thanks, Johnnie, for the backhanded compliment.

The Luncheon Voucher Madam

One evening I was at Charing Cross Station when Cynthia Payne got in the cab. Cynthia ran a brothel at her house in Streatham for older professional punters who could pay for services with luncheon vouchers! Such was her fame that her activities became the subject of a film called 'Professional Services' starring Julie Walters as Cynthia. This particular evening she was giving an after dinner speech at the Dorchester. I found her to be a lovely aunt-type of woman. She paid me, asking my name. Then she out of her purse got a business card with her kipper on the front. On the back she wrote: 'Dear Roger, thanks for all your past custom. Love, Cynthia'.

A different and nice line, but hardly a card to be shown to the missus!

Andy Williams

I was having a night out with four fellow cab drivers and their wives at Michael Caine's restaurant Langans in

Mayfair when Andy Williams came in after doing a show at the Barbican. As he walked past our table, I spoke to him and he stopped and had a glass of champagne with us. He was chatty and the men saw that it was obvious he was interested in the women at the table, which we took as compliment to our taste in the ladies. Of course, the ladies, all done up to the nines, were all flattered and went back relaying the story to the mums collecting their kids on Monday afternoon after school.

Rod Stewart

One Saturday night I was in St James Street with four lovely ladies in their twenties in the back of the cab. I was sitting in traffic when a large Hummer with tinted windows pulled alongside the cab. The window came down and a blonde mop of hair shouted, "Which way to Mount Street, driver?"

The four ladies all started to scream, and I couldn't hear myself giving directions to Rod the God.

"Thanks, pal!" and he was gone into the night, leaving my fares rather aroused.

Colonel Comb Over

A favourite place for cabmen to eat at night was the Fryer's Delight, a fish and chip shop opposite Holborn Police Station in Theobald's Road. It was always full with eighty percent of its clientele cab drivers. One night in came Arthur Scargill, wearing a sailor type of hat, with some company. The cafe had mirrors all along the wall. Arthur took off his hat and re-arranged his comb over hair carefully in the mirror a la Bobby Charlton. I couldn't resist a wolf whistle, which produced lots of laughter and left Arthur red faced.

World's Most Beautiful Women

It is not often men can brag they have been in the company of some of the most beautiful women in the world, albeit there was a glass partition between us. Beauty is in the eye of the beholder and for me, these are the most beautiful women I have ever had the pleasure to drive. I have never forgotten them or the fare.

Julie Christie - Baker Street to Hamleys toyshop;

Nanette Newman - Kings Road to Berkley Square;

Bianca Jagger - Bond Street to Portman Square;

Lee Remick - Hilton to St Johns Wood;

Joan Collins - Maida Vale to Mayfair.

And my favourite, for whom I had a thing for ever since I saw her in 'Gigi': Leslie Caron, from Harrods to Kensington.

Yes, I can still smell their perfume!

Celeb Disappointments

Not all celebs want to talk to hairy arsed cab drivers, but it doesn't hurt to be polite. I always backed off after the second knock back and left them to their own company. In all my years in the cab, I only remember two disappointments, perhaps because I caught them on a bad day and I expected better of them.

Jonathan Ross

It was a rainy Sunday afternoon in the West End and he asked for a tiny street in Kentish Town, and I was pleased that I knew it. Didn't want any conversation and paid the exact fare. No tip. I believe he is of working class stock, but definitely not "one of your own."

Sir Alec Guinness

As a kid I loved all the old black and white British films, and Alec Guinness in particular, was a favourite actor of mine. He wanted to go from Victoria to Leith's Restaurant on Kensington Park Road, probably a twenty minute job. After two attempts at conversation met with only a smile, I gave up. He sat with an umbrella between his legs and both hands on top of the brolly, looking rather grand and military. Perhaps he was re-enacting his Oscar-winning role in 'Bridge Over the River Kwai'.

Gays

Homosexuality was illegal in the UK until 1967, but humans of all persuasions need a place to socialise. When I was a kid in the fifties we were aware there were gay members of the community and of the pubs and clubs that were frequented predominately by them. As a driver, I was always comfortable with gays as long as they kept themselves to themselves. In the still of the night, driving through London, I always liked their humour and they never gave any trouble, only too pleased to get home safe in a cab instead of the all-night buses with the drunks and trouble.

On one night, two queens got in at Olympia. Both were a bit 'Brahms and Liszt'.

"Driver, are you gay?"

"Gay? I'm not even happy."

Dorothy and Toto

Four young men got in at Earl's Court and one, sitting on the pull down seat engaged me in conversation. After a while he said, "In another life I'd like to be Dorothy in 'The Wizard of Oz'. Those beautiful shoes, oh!"

The conversation went on and I said something that amused him. He turned to the back seat and said, "Did you hear what the driver said?"

His pal, obviously miffed, said, "He's your friend, not mine."

Chelsea Kilt

At the back of Chelsea's football ground is a cemetery that became a gathering place for men at night. A hand went up and I saw a blonde with shoulder length hair, a mini skirt with stockings and suspenders below the hem line. I pulled in and looked at the 'boat race' and spied more stubble on the face than there should be. In a broad Scottish accent he said, "West Kensington Station, pal." When he got out, he walked away on high heels like a Dick Emery impersonation.

Strangest Request

The weirdest request I ever had was when a young man asked would I come in, tie him up and beat him up. When I declined his request, he offered me money to do it. I drove away thinking there were homophobes who would do it willingly without payment, but I expect they would be looking at police charges.

Toff Tales

Toffy is a rich man, toffy is a snob.
Toffy doesn't like it if you call him Brother Bob.

Meriam Webster's Dictionary provides more than a few definitions of a 'gentleman', the foremost being "a man who treats other people in a proper and polite way; a man whose conduct conforms to a high standard of propriety and behaviour"; and curiously, a third definition is "a man of any social class or condition". For the British, fewer things are more important than polite and courteous behaviour. The irony is, the British class system conspires to undermine the rules of expected behaviour. And never more visible is this than in the relationship of driver to passenger when the passenger in question is, to be frank, someone you would expect to know better, but for some reason behave, as if they are better, smarter or more important than other people. And worse, when their condescending attitude comes with the presumption that their career, station, wealth or position in life gives them the right to treat their fellow human beings as little more than menial labour that exist to do their bidding.

Sadly, boorish, not to mention violently abusive behaviour, towards cabbies is not a bygone thing of 50 years ago. Fairly recently, a retired physicist and member of the Royal Institution admitted assault causing actual bodily harm by "hitting a taxi driver over the head with a walking stick because he feared he was going to be late to the opera". Also, not to forget the recent foul-mouthed rant by a former Cabinet Minister at a cabbie who happened to annoy him.

So, sadly, driving wasn't all jolly fun and yes, I've had my fair share of what I call the "Mark I No Spares". You can't avoid them altogether. A 'Mark I No Spares', is an easily recognised type, distinguished by old school tie with cut away shirt collar, watch chain from buttonhole on lapel into top pocket, striped business suit with thick brogues, and sporting a brolly and the older fifties version of bowler hat. They always speak with a public school accent, and sometimes display disdain for the so-called lower classes.

The following are my own encounters with the type.

My First Encounter with a Posh Boy

Sometime in 1957 I was entered for the Duke of Edinburgh's Award by the Bradfield Boys Club in Peckham. This excursion was to see if I was capable of surviving a weekend in the countryside, travelling on foot from Point A to Point B, living in a tent. The London boys were teamed up with a public school boy for two days and dropped off from the bus in pairs at intervals on the South Downs. For my sins, I inherited one Nicholas Double-Barrelled Whatever as my co-adventurer, who hailed from Putney.

On the day, it is teaming with rain. The coach pulls away, leaving us in a country lane with a tent to be erected. Nicholas is standing there with his bins all steamed up and looking very nervous. Remember, we are both 15, the same age, and remember I always thought it was the upper class johnnies took charge in times of stress.

The said Nicholas starts crying. I think to myself, how did I end up with this NANCY? For a while, we sat under a big tree, sheltering from the downpour, until we got our thoughts together. He tells me that his 'pater' wanted him to come on this sortie to 'make him a man'. All my Dad had said to me was "Enjoy yourself" and "Got enough money, son?"

Now, anyone who knows me recognises that I am not mechanically minded, but, regardless, I begin to put the tent up in some woods. Nicholas stands there, *just stands there*, watching, until I scream at him, "For fuck's sake, hold this pole up!" Oh great. He starts blubbing again. "I don't want to be here!" he whimpers. I didn't tell him, but I would rather have spent the night in the tent with a smelly penny stamp.

All my effort was in vain. We made it to the finishing line on the second day only to be told by an officer from Sandhurst that we had cheated. Apparently, one of the objectives was to cook and fend for ourselves in the outback. As it happened, just off a minor road, I had spotted a small café and, taking what I considered was initiative and showing not a little ingenuity under the circumstances, enjoyed a fry up with Little Lord Fauntleroy. Unfortunately, we were seen by observers, lying in wait.

All in all I look back now and laugh. Nicholas Double-Barrelled Whatever probably finished up a Top Johnnie in the Government. The posh boys run the country, the working class make it work.

All Men are Equal, Aren't They?

It was about 6pm and I dropped off at the Reform Club in Pall Mall, when up comes a toff with enough waves in his hair to make him seasick. He told me to wait while he said cheerio to a foreign-looking 'ice cream'.

After a couple of minutes of fare-the-wells, he came up to the window.

"Where to, mate?" I said

He got in and said, "Café Royal. And please don't address me as 'mate'".

I laughed at his haughty manner and got the hump with him.

He purred, "Do you know who I just left? It was the brother of the Sultan of Brunei."

I think this was meant to impress me.

"I'd be more impressed if it was Winston Churchill, mate."

"Why are you so rude? I would prefer you called me 'Sir'."

I replied, "Of all the thousands of fares I've picked up, not one has objected to my calling them 'mate'. Perhaps it's something in your snobbish attitude to the supposed lower classes."

Then I asked, "Would you call me 'Sir', mate?"

"No, I wouldn't."

"Why?"

"Because you are a cab driver" a remark that told me more than anything of his upper class breeding and disdain for the common chap.

I pulled up outside the Café Royal, and he went to get his wallet out, but before he could offer me the fare I said, "Poke the money up your arse you conceited mug" and drove off.

All men are equal, aren't they, mate?

Mastermind

A few years back the 'London Evening Standard' carried a story that a London cab driver had bigger brains than other people because of the amount of knowledge they needed for their job. All the wags were taking the 'pee' from the back of the cab and after a few weeks, it was wearing a bit thin. One day, a 'Mark I No Spares' gets in the cab of a pal of mine and begins the fare to the City.

"I hear all you chappies have an enlarged brain, then why aren't you in a better job. Ha ha."

My pal had had enough. "Okay, let's see how clever you are. Who said 'we will fight them on the beaches'?"

"Oh, so easy," says Mark I. "Winston Churchill."

"Who said 'I shall return'?"

Easy peasy. "General McArthur."

"Who said 'There's no profit in defeat'?"

"I say, that's difficult. I don't know," says Pinstripe. "Who did say there's no profit in defeat?"

"A Jamaican chiropodist."

With that, he closed the connecting window and was silent for the rest of the journey. Needless to say my pal got a 'George Segal': in the cab trade's jargon 'No tip'.

Mousetrap!

One night, just about theatre time, a hand went up as I went along Fulham Broadway. It was a 'Mark I' and his horsey 'gel'.

"The Mousetrap as quick as you can!" he ordered. No

please, no thank you, not so much as a kiss my arse. I put the ignorance down to his youth.

I did tear about to get them to the longest running play in the West End. An Agatha Christie whodunit, it always plays to packed houses at St Martin's Theatre, Covent Garden, which is just off Charing Cross Road.

I got them there in good time before curtain call.

Now, whenever I get service, I always tip, and this fare, in my book, deserved, at best, a couple of shills after my tearing about for them.

"How much, driver?" said Mark I.

"Twelve shillings sixpence, please mate."

I got a 'George Segal' – the exact fare.

"Oh lovely, much obliged," I said sarcastically.

"Have I upset you, driver?" asked Mark I.

"No, mate, but I'll upset you – it was the butler wot dun it!"

The 'Slurry' Solicitor

It was about 10.45pm as we all came out of the restaurant on Waterloo Road. Six of us were standing alongside a cab, just chewing the fat, before we went once more into the fray. Along came an old fashioned-looking 'ice cream' with a trilby 'tit' and a battered raincoat carrying a briefcase. He was about forty years old and by the tone of his voice was very well educated.

"Who's for hire?" he asked.

"Where are you going?" a voice enquired, aiming to determine who this fare might help on the driver's way home.

"Ewell, in Surrey," he said.

They all looked at me because I was the only one who lived south.

"That cab there," I said, pointing to my cab.

As we set out, he told me he was a solicitor and was in a hurry to get home, and I sussed he had been drinking. As the journey went on, he became more and more argumentative about the cab drivers he had come across. I wasn't entertaining his philosophy. I think the final straw for him was when I said, "If the country was run like the cab trade it would be on its feet tomorrow."

"How's that?" he enquired.

"No malingerers. We all do an honest day's work and live or die on our performance. If we don't go to work, the baby doesn't get fed or the mortgage paid."

"Rubbish," he said, without any reasoning.

By now, I wanted to give him either a volley of abuse or an uppercut.

We came off the Kingston Bypass and he began to give me instructions, as would a sergeant major on the parade ground to young cadets, "Left here. Right here. Straight over." And not a please or a thank you or a kiss my arse.

We arrived at the street where he lived and he insisted I pull up outside his house. It was a busy road so I had to wait to do a U-turn. Meantime, he continued aggravating, urging me "Just go on over there."

"I will when it's safe," I said.

I'm finally able to U-turn. He got out and slammed the door, putting the exact fare through the window and demanding a receipt for the trip so he can claim it back from his company. I wrote the receipt out and smiled,

"Thank you and good night."

I was off down the road like the number six dog at Walthamstow race track, furtively looking in the mirror behind me. I saw Mr Obnoxious in the road calling after me. He who laughs last, laughs longest: the only detail on his receipt was a single word – 'bollocks'.

Eartha Kitt

Every Friday we always ate in Camden Town in a Greek Restaurant called the Kolossi Castle with a table for eight at the back of the place near the kitchen. It was a family-run restaurant: mum, dad and two sons. We were always well looked after, with plenty olives, chillies, hummus and pitta bread. The only problem for me was sometimes the food worked out a bit lively, and about 2 am I was looking for a toilet.

About midnight, after our meal, I was in Soho, when an 'ice cream' put his hand up and wanted to go out to the stockbroker belt in Surrey, a trip that would take about fifty minutes. He was a nice man, and directed me off the motorway to a real fancy, old style private estate: lamps on top of the entrance, big detached houses, which today would be worth about £1.5 million, possibly £2 million.

Unfortunately, 'el greco' I'd eaten was bothering me, and I knew I wouldn't make it back to London to find a clean toilet at that time of the morning.

So, having lots of McDonald's napkins in my cab, I pull out of the estate, pull over in a quiet lane, in total darkness at the side of a ditch, and at the back wheel of the cab I crouched down (please note, under the laws in the Hackney Carriage it's okay to pee). I finished my business, when a big Labrador runs up to me barking. Its master strolled up asking if all was well. Thinking quick, I said, "Just changed the tyre, mate, thanks for asking."

"Good night, driver, safe journey home."

Toby and Jemima

Early morning. It was snowing. I was in Royal Hospital Road, Chelsea when a 'Mark I No Spares' and his horsey lady, scarf tied under chin, hailed the cab. He was the double of James Hewitt. He sported a beautiful camel hair military-style overcoat with a brown velvet collar. She was a typical Sloane Ranger of the type normally seen at horse riding shows and in earlier years, at debutante balls.

"Ennismore Gardens."

No please, no thank you.

He pulled down the little seat and put his wet, muddy brogues on the leather. I never took any notice.

We got to Sloane Avenue and he started whistling to get my attention, "Hey, hey."

"Are you talking to me?" I said, in my best De Niro/Travis Bickle imitation.

"Yes, I am."

"Do me a favour, mate. No more whistling. Only dogs answer to whistles."

"I've changed my mind. Go to Beauchamp Place."

Once again, no 'please'.

And to add insult to injury he added, "Get on with it" and gave another couple of whistles.

I stopped the cab on a tanner. "Out. This cab won't take you anywhere!"

"You are not getting paid, you little shit."

She chimes in with, "Oh, Toby, don't be silly. I'll pay you, driver."

"Don't you dare pay him, Jemima. My father is a barrister and knows how to deal with the likes of him."

I said, "You can tell your father that when you knock the driver for the fare, it's called a 'bilk'."

By now, I'm out of the cab and taking Jemima's money, thanking her. He completely loses the plot, goes to the back of the cab, and takes down the cab number and the plate number on a piece of paper. He then rips off my cab badge that was hanging from the top button of the pink Lacoste I'm wearing, plants a right-hander to the bridge of my nose, and proceeds to walk away with my badge in his hand. My nose is pouring blood and now I lose the plot. I want to do him badly.

As a cab driver, you can't start the affray but you can defend yourself.

I spin him round by his brown velvet collar and gave him a Glasgow kiss. We are on top of a car's bonnet and he is pulling my hair out with both hands. Very invitingly, his nose is inches away from my mouth: with top and bottom set, I spring into action. He screams like a stuck pig. I am now on top of him on the floor, giving him a few right handers and Jemima is screaming for me to stop.

Another cab driver pulled me off. I kicked him up the 'Khyber', and the duo walk into the night. I picked up my cab badge from the pavement.

A police car pulled up. I made the blood look worse than it was by rubbing the blood on both hands.

"I've been attacked."

An old man came forward and said, "I saw it all, Officer. The cabbie was attacked."

The policeman asked if I was okay and left.

The old boy said, "I'll go witness for you. Any chance of running me to Bayswater?"

Not wishing to alienate my witness, I didn't charge him.

The next day I went to Millwall with my Dad with two black eyes and a swollen nose. I smiled to myself, picturing the scene in Toby's local trendy wine bar: "What's wrong with your nose, Toby?"

"Oh, a cabbie tried to bite it orrfff!"

CHAPTER TEN
LTDA -
Licensed Taxi Drivers' Association

I loved driving a cab: I was my own boss, started and finished when I liked, fixed in time to go to football, play squash and spend time with my family. I visited my parents three times a week, taking my kids when they were young. I was happy with my life but then I became aware of the shortcomings of a cab driver's lot. I knew if I was to stay for the rest of my working days, change was needed.

I read books about Jack Dash (dockers), Arthur Scargill (miners), Jimmy Hoffa (American teamsters), and already did a correspondence course at Ruskin College on Trade Unionism. I started attending branch meetings of a newly formed group called the Licensed Taxi Drivers Association. At that time there were four divisions: North-East, South-East, South-West and North-West. Depending on where you lived, you attended the meetings and could put forward motions to be resolved and ratified by the others.

My branch was South-East, and having read a book called 'Lord Citrine's Book on Chairmanship', I attended a meeting above a pub in Camberwell Green called the Sterling Castle. I didn't know what to expect. It was certainly an eye opener. The Chairman couldn't control the thirty or so drivers but what I did recognise was that there were kindred spirits who wanted what I wanted.

We wanted better ranks; benefits through the Association; good legal representation when in jeopardy of losing your livelihood; and changes to the Hackney Carriage laws. For example in the sixties we did not feel it was necessary to carry a bale of hay for horses! I wasn't any different to the rest of the drivers, except I tried to be constructive, did not shout, and used my newly acquired 'point of order' or 'point of information' which impressed the meeting.

At my first meeting I remember a tall man, well dressed, sitting at the back of the hall. He raised his hand to speak. I thought this will be constructive. Referring to our incumbent Council of Management for the LTDA he said "What they need is a squib up their arses" and sat down to cries of "here, here".

Within two monthly meetings, I was elected to Secretary of the Branch. After four meetings I was elected Chairman. Being Chairman of the South-East Branch gave me the right to attend the monthly Council of Management (COM) meetings and to represent our branch.

The COM was made up of ten elected drivers plus four area branch chairmen and was held at the Paddington headquarters of the LTDA once a month.

At my first meeting I participated, but mainly to suss out the strengths and weaknesses of my fellow committee men.

I was thirty two years old and the youngest around the table. The committee all had the best intentions for the cab trade but didn't always know the road to take. If you don't know where you're going, any road will do. My branch loaded the bullets and I fired the gun, both barrels at any offending or errant elected member of the COM.

I started attending the other three branches to see if they felt the same as my branch, wanting change. The North-East branch (East End) was in step, the South-West branch, although low in numbers were also the same. The only branch not too keen to lead on with the forward thinking was the North-West. They were a much older group, puffing on pipes, had been driving for many years and weren't looking for much change as they were facing retirement and the big cab rank in the sky.

My maiden speech with the COM, outlining the changes my branch wanted was greeted by "All well and good. What's the learned Chairman going to do to bring about these changes?" sounding more than a little sarcastic.

'At the next election I am going to stand for office and will base my campaign on what I will offer the trade.'

There were three full time jobs: General Secretary, Chairman and legal representative at the time. The Treasurer was a part-time job and the other positions were part-time and paid stand down pay in lieu of cab takings.

The LTDA was in a sorry financial state and was barely ticking over. It had five hundred members and was living hand to mouth. It had a cab garage, an insurance brokerage, a legal department, a trade newspaper and a radio work circuit. None of them were exactly setting the world on fire financially, despite the right ideas of the General Secretary, Bill D'Arcy, a man of principle and good wishes.

It is worth noting that other than attending COM meetings from which you received minimal pay, all visits to the Paddington offices to discuss association business were not paid and were in your own time.

So once again before I went to sleep I closed my eyes, not to dream of Raquel Welch or Jane Fonda, but ways I could benefit my mates and grow an Association that could take care of us.

It was standard practice that if a driver died, a couple of his pals would get buckets and collect at the stations for his widow and kids. The cab trade, being generous, would throw in money on the way to the taxi rank. All this was well and good if the deceased was well known and a face in the trade. If the departed wasn't liked or not well known the response was still good but not as good as those known and well-liked. It was not a level playing field.

I lost a good friend in Jimmy Kray who took a heart attack and died. Together with another pal, Tony Lock, we spent the day at Waterloo Station collecting for Jim's missus and son. After that day I decided that through the Association all men should get the same deal as a right, via their monthly dues.

Tony Lock, a good pal and fellow traveler, to better the cab trade's lot

I spent endless nights trying to work out what I could do to get life cover *en bloc* along with sickness pay. My initial idea was to work out how many drivers I needed to make it viable through the LTDA and keep the profits made by the underwriters to plough back in benefits to the members. In the end I succumbed to the orthodox way.

I contacted insurance companies and got monthly figures for sick pay and life cover. The insurers were giving good rates, but I had to produce 4,000 drivers before these rates would apply. I said I could produce the numbers but wanted three months to get them in. I got the time, and went to the Council at a special meeting to discuss the proposal.

I had done my sums and presented a new monthly subscription for the LTDA. In it was built a contingency fund which would pay any bills for drivers badly incapacitated. A sickness payment kicked in after two weeks and ran for one hundred and four weeks; life cover was included. I also built in a pound a month profit to run the LTDA. This was 1976.

This new innovation was called the 'A' scheme. For those not interested they could belong to the 'B' scheme at a much reduced rate and which gave them access to the work radio, legal department and garage.

The COM accepted the proposal but had reservations I could deliver 4,000 members. So did I, but I wasn't showing any lack of confidence. As Walt Disney said *'All our dreams can come true – if we have the courage to pursue them.'*

I had the COM's permission to launch the scheme, utilised the printing facilities and agreed the offer of the insurance company.

The scheme was launched. Each driver had an application form to fill in for either 'A' or 'B' scheme to commence three months from the launch date. I went to the office every day to open the post and to speak with any driver with questions. I went to all branch meetings which were greatly attended, to answer some of the doubting Thomas'.

I did all I could to get support.

The pressure on me was heavy to say the least, and when I was under the cosh my forehead broke out in a big rash which spread to either side of my nose. Still not getting any 'Nelson Eddies', I had to leave the office and work into the night on the cab.

After the first month, I had over 2,500 replies.

After the second month, I had over 3,200 replies.

At the end of the third month it was a done deal – 4,222 replies received in total.

I was weeks away from producing my manifesto for the COM elections. I wrote about the new benefits and other ideas I wanted to introduce.

The elections were for a three-year tenure, and I got a good vote. At the first meeting of the COM the newly elected Committee voted me in as treasurer full-time. I needed a welfare officer and Bill Thorpe, who worked with me to get the 'A' scheme off the ground and who also got elected to the Council, got the job. He visited the drivers at home and came back with any bills that couldn't be met, bringing the contingency fund into play.

The 'A' scheme needed to be policed and if Bill Thorpe felt someone was playing us off, we would plot up and survey. The penalty for cheating your fellow cab drivers was paying back the cash and expulsion from the LTDA. A cheater would have to be caught before being banged to rights: we would follow, see a pick up and drop off, and even photograph it, leaving little defence.

Every year our track record would be reviewed by the insurer, and if bad, our premiums would go up. We couldn't afford for a good thing to be abused.

I had many sleepless nights at the beginning, but I am delighted to say that after thirty-five years the benefits are still there for the members. Over the years hundreds of families have been assisted financially because they had the insight to put their money up and support the 'A' scheme collectively.

You are only as good as your last fight, so I couldn't rest on my laurels.

'What happens when the two years' of sick pay runs out' was a regular question. Once again I went to the insurance companies to get a quote for permanent health insurance (PHI). At our negotiations for sickness cover at Lloyds, I was taken to lunch by two 'Mark One' public school boys, who found me amusing, looking down their noses. Did I have the last laugh? After they drew up the contract, and only when both parties signed it, did I reveal their glaring error. Instead of quoting for a monthly fee, which was what had been agreed, the document quoted for *quarterly payment* at the same price. The LTDA need the money desperately at that time, but after two quarters, I relented and adhered to the monthly payments.

The PHI provided sick cover until you departed life but there was a deferred period before it kicked in, and was

TALES FROM THE RANKS AND BEYOND | 321

Harry Feigen and Bill Thorpe, LTDA, and Two League of Mutual Taxi Owners (LOMTO), New York officials in white shirts

A meeting with the Taxi Commissioner (white coat) in New York, 1979

offered as an optional extra not as an integral part of the monthly dues. For anybody wanting a pension we brought in Norwich Union at a group rate, and again this was optional.

We also started a monthly lottery long before the National Lottery and built a gym for the drivers in the basement of our headquarters.

Now, no one was afraid to speak to our bank manager. In fact, once a quarter I went to lunch with the top man at Williams and Glyn's in his dining room in Lombard Street to discuss our cash flow problems with the radio company, which became the biggest in London. The drivers needed paying for their credit work, and the bigger the company the longer you waited for payment from the big conglomerates. The CEO of the bank was a gentleman who understood and at times we were talking in millions.

In 1979 I introduced the facility of a credit union to the London licensed trade. In Great Britain in 1978 there were no taxi credit unions, and I had read about the League of Mutual Taxi Owners (LMTO) in New York. The LMTO had their own credit union since 1934 and provided an avenue for their members to become taxi owners through the credit union. At the time, the taxi plate, shaped like a 'big apple' was valued at $100,000. I wanted to see how I could adopt it for London.

As there is no plate value in London, unlike other major cities like Glasgow or Edinburgh, I was looking to get credit union loans for cab purchase. What was the big attraction? 12.68% APR, 1% on the outstanding balance a month. So basically it meant that if you borrowed, say, £100 you would repay £10 in the first month and £1 interest. Second month, you'd have £90 outstanding and repay £10 with 90p interest and so on.

The other benefits were that when a member died, his shares and savings were doubled to his next of kin and his loan cancelled, dependent on age.

I was treated royally by my New York counterparts and for several years after invited to be guest speaker at their credit union annual general meeting in the Catskills, all expenses paid.

To form a credit union in Great Britain you had to apply to the Register of Friendly Societies (RFS), based in Great Marlborough Street next to the stage door of the London Palladium. The stipulation of the RFS was that there had

Picket line against Mann and Overton's rapid price increases

to be a common bond between its members. Our common bond was membership of the LTDA.

Another benefit was that any person living at the member's address could also join. It was getting better. Husband, wife, kids over eighteen, grandad etc. - all were eligible to join.

Having had a run-in with Mann and Overton, the sole distributor of cabs in London, over their heavy increases in the price of cabs every six months, the LTDA put a picket line at their factory until they agreed to play the game.

At the branch meetings I attended each month there always would be, at various intervals the hardy annual question of the executive salaries. After a while I had my standard reply in gear and never departed from it: "Some people have short memories. I don't remember you questioning salaries when I worked for minimal stand down pay to set up the various benefits that you receive today. If you look at the wages that the executive receives you will see that it is very close to the figure that every one of you earn. I want what I could earn on a cab, why should my family suffer because I am in service to the membership. The only difference is that I get holiday pay and get to wear a suit to work, which comes in handy when I represent you on TV or with government officials."

Usually the above was enough to keep the troops happy.

It was never easy at branch meetings, especially the South-East and the North-East who were the more vociferous. The South-East was my branch and I got a lot of backing. I remember one night when I was at a big meeting. There was a big man, with a big mouth, who kept shouting abuse to the top table. I stood up and pointed at him, 'Have I seen you on the telly?' You could hear a pin drop.

'No,' he said guardedly.

'You sure?' I enquired.

'No,' he repeated.

The meeting waited for the punch line.

'I'm sure I have,' I said. 'Interference, please put your hand up and follow procedure.'

The meeting laughed and Big Mouth was very sheepish for the duration of the meeting.

One of the LTDA annual benefits was a golf tournament for the members. The main prize was a brand new car for any driver getting a hole in one on a par three in the afternoon. The sponsors put up many prizes but the car was the big one.

In the morning round a good guy and fellow Millwall man, Ron Vosper, got a hole in one on the specified hole. Despite the overtures made to the sponsors, they were adamant they stipulated the afternoon round. A good day was had by all but no amount of booze on the nineteenth hole could cheer Ron up.

Driving home from the LTDA I passed the Old Vic Theatre in Waterloo, and the name of one of the cast rang a bell. It took about thirty minutes for the penny to drop. We had a driver off sick with back problems for several weeks and he was drawing benefit. On closer investigation it was the same man. In the rules it stated that other occupations to supplement your income were not allowed. The benefit was only to cover your sole income of driving a cab.

When the actor was called to headquarters it turned out he was earning more a week at the Old Vic than he could have earned on his cab. The Council decided he had flouted the rules and he was taken off sick benefit immediately. There were no complaints from the thespian.

Back problems are an 'iffy' area: it can never be totally proved. And although our budding Olivier couldn't sit behind the wheel of a cab, he was okay for two shows a day treading the boards at a prestigious theatre.

My main employment as Treasurer of the Executive Association was finances, but other chores often came up. The Association negotiated with the Public Carriage Office that drivers could wear tailored shorts in the summertime, and drivers were informed in our trade newspaper. They were delighted with this addition to the dress code because air conditioning was non-existent.

One morning about 6.30am, I was awakened by a telephone call from one of the men on the Southeast Committee, complaining about the doorman at the Hilton Hotel in Park Lane, Mayfair. Apparently, this doorman was taking 'the bung' from Private Hire drivers for airport jobs, leaving the leftovers to the licensed trade. When drivers are 'on point' on a taxi rank, they take their job whatever the destination, be it good, bad or indifferent. I instructed my committeeman to boycott all pickups until I got there. I arrived at Park Lane to see a large queue for taxis, people eager to get away to business or travel. The doorman was identified to me. I went into the hotel forecourt, introduced myself to the manager and threatened a seven day boycott. I explained the situation to the manager, who placated me with promises that it wouldn't occur again. Of course it happened again, and became an ongoing battle.

Being a loose cannon, I was often kept away from negotiations at the Home Office, especially when the Tories were in power. On one occasion when I attended a meeting at the Home Office, I remember the incumbent Home Secretary, a Tory public school boy, stating, "When I travel to London, I see big houses with cabs on the drive. How do they afford it?" Before my chairman could stop me, I replied, "If a man does an honest day's work, surely he can provide his family with a nice lifestyle. Or is that only the preserve of the upper classes? I doubt if many of your colleagues would want to drive a cab in all weathers, in the worst traffic in Great Britain, surrounded by petrol fumes for eight hours a day."

The Home Secretary nodded and smiled, but unfortunately, I wasn't finished with him yet. As the meeting progressed, he suggested that the animal charge should be dropped from the meter. At the time, any dog or cat in the back of the cab warranted sixpence or a one shilling (I can't remember which) surcharge on the meter. Asking what our reply would be to the abolition of the animal charge, I replied, "This will not be received too well by the drivers on the cab ranks on a Saturday afternoon at Millwall, West Ham or Chelsea. It will reduce their income."

Your man never got it, and I was never taken back to Whitehall again. To this day, I've never favoured the 'softly, softly' approach

"I Am Not Myself Westminster Elite"
Whether be it for good or ill, I have to say that self-employment exacerbated my natural streak of resistance to authority. I would not then, or now, tolerate either the smug or the arrogant, full of their own self-importance,

barking orders or looking down from the metaphorical perch. No one 'takes a liberty' as Grandad was wont to say, and certainly not where it threatened a man's right to earn a decent livelihood.

The cab trade had not had a fare increase for about five years, and there was great deal of anti-government feeling. The Home Office were authorised to negotiate with the representatives of the cab trade for pay awards on the meter, but they were not playing the game. So one Wednesday afternoon in the Paddington office of the LTDA, the Council of Management decided to take action. The four-man Executive proposed a Sunday afternoon drive-in at Whitehall to express the trade's disgust at our poor treatment from Jim Callaghan's boys. It took place on 29 October 1978.

The word spread for drivers to head for either Parliament Square or Trafalgar Square and to drive slowly down Whitehall at a specified time. Drivers turned out in their hundreds, with families in the back. That part of London came to a standstill. The Executive hired our operations room above a pub at the top of Whitehall and were delighted with the response from the troops. One driver was playing in his jazz band, and another wore a gorilla suit saying 'Pay peanuts, you get monkeys'.

Whitehall vintage cab en route to number 10 with a heavily signed petition

Prior to the drive-in, we stationed a vintage cab near the entrance of Downing Street. When the time was right, the Executive drove the cab to Number Ten with a petition signed by thousands of London licensed taxi drivers.

The police were completely taken by surprise and unable to cope, but it was all good humoured. As soon as we handed in the petition, the cabs went away as quickly as they came.

At a subsequent meeting with the Home Office, it was tentatively agreed that it would be in the public's interest to have a one and a half percent to two percent increase, based on the operation costs for taxis, rather than a five-year delay, resulting in a ten percent increase on the clock. Obviously, this resulted in customer resistance. Whereas, back then, one shilling or two shillings wouldn't be too bitter a pill to swallow for cab users. All London cab drivers are self-employed and should never be asked to strike. Boycotts or drive-ins were or best tools, which we amply displayed on a wonderful day in Whitehall.

After the tariff increase for the London licensed cab trade, I represented the LTDA at the BBC to be interviewed on radio about the fare hike. I went to Portland Place and was shown into a reception room where to my delight was a comic hero of mine, Norman Wisdom, dressed in a reefer jacket and a jaunty sailor's hat. We shook hands and I told him how much my parents loved his films because they didn't have to hear to appreciate the actions and pratfalls. A top man. Then I was called into a studio and I knew what was waiting. After a short preamble about the meter increase, the interviewer asked, "How much does a London cab driver earn?"

Being cognisant of the hundreds of fellow drivers whom I knew would be listening, I gave my standard reply.

"Not possible to generalise, how long is a piece of string? There are older drivers living in council accommodation who work short shifts and rent their cabs a couple of days a week. On the other hand, there are young guys with new cabs and their own properties in the suburbs. Every cab driver works to his personal requirements."

After several more questions, I was free to go. When I walked past the cab rank outside the BBC, an older cab driver tooted his horn and gave me the thumbs up. Job done.

The Nearly Man

At a Council of Management meeting of the LTDA, it was proposed, seconded and carried out that I was to be the next General Secretary. Harry Feigen, the incumbent, asked for me to let him see his term of office out, which was not a problem as I respected Harry and had a lot of time for him. Meanwhile, fate conspired against me and I never got the job I always coveted.

The LTDA Credit Union was going great guns and other associational and industrial groups wanting to start a credit union made contact to see how feasible it was for them. At the time, our credit union had received good coverage from top newspapers. I was invited to speak at various conferences, usually in the north of England: Blackpool, Scarborough and Skegness. I had got the credit union bug.

There were a few problems with our radio company, and I was following up claims from the drivers that work jobs were given illegally. The drivers loaded the gun and I fired the bullets. Basically, it was two camps with different views, with the drivers against the board and staff of the radio company. I received threatening telephone calls in the middle of the night from the control room telling me to back off. I ignored the cowards who wouldn't be identified or face me up.

It was all hands to the pump. In addition to managing a lottery for the drivers and being in conflict with various elements of the radio company, the sickness scheme needed re-negotiation and the credit union was growing by leaps and bounds. I was spending all too few hours at home and getting stressed, very stressed.

Then, out of the blue, I was made an offer I couldn't refuse.

ABCUL (Association of British Credit Unions Ltd)

I was exhausted and at an all-time low, possibly on the border of a break-down, when the knock came on the door for me

```
NNNN



02 JUN 1987/1923
ZCZC DLM0155 NKY890 IOB300 1-005604I153
GBXX CO UDNX 069
TDMX BRIDGETON MO 69/65 02 1317




ROGER LEWIS
LICENSED TAXI DRIVERS ASSN
9/11 WOODFIELD ROAD
LONDONW92BAENGLAND



FROM TELEX 467918
MADISON, WISCONSIN
JUNE 2, 1987



CONGRATULATIONS YOUR APPOINTMENT AS ABCUL CEO.  POSITION WILL
BE A REAL CHALLENGE AND IS OF TREMENDOUS IMPORTANCE TO FUTURE
OF CREDIT UNIONS IN GREAT BRITAIN.  WE AT THE WORLD COUNCIL
LOOK FORWARD TO WORKING WITH YOU AS YOU UNDERTAKE YOUR NEW
RESPONSIBILITIES.


BEST WISHES


SCHUMACHER/WOCCU



COL  9/11 W9 2BA 467918 2, 1987
```

to reply to an advertisement in a top newspaper for the job of CEO for ABCUL. I don't think there were too many horses in the race, because, at the time, on our shores the credit union was a well-kept secret. After all, I had to go to New York to find another cab drivers' union to pick brains.

I went for an interview at a head hunter's company and was completely swayed and flattered by the salary and conditions offered. I remember thinking, in the cab going home from the interview, if I got the job it wasn't too shabby for a boy with a different upbringing, born into a silent world and living above a junk yard. I remember thinking how proud my Mum and Dad would be.

The job meant representing Great Britain at World Council Meetings, negotiating with the Registry of Friendly Societies, growing the membership by speaking at various conferences, servicing the existing members and promoting the ideals of the worldwide movement.

On 2 June 1987, I received the following telegram (telegram from ABCUL).

With great trepidation, I resigned my position with the LTDA. I loved the Association but felt that I had gone as far as I could. I left the Association in a good financial position, with a fine membership figure and ongoing benefits for the members. There was no going back. To this day, twenty-eight years later, I have never been back, but I live with the knowledge that thousands of London licensed cab drivers have had the benefit of my insight.

My love of the credit union movement and concept will always remain with me. Unfortunately, my appointment as CEO for ABCUL was not always going to be sweetness and light. I was my own man.

The Cuna Mutual Insurance Company in America had underwritten the British Credit Union movement since it was formed and were looking to break into profit at some stage. It was a numbers game, and we needed to develop a growing association, with community, associational and industrial credit unions paying subscriptions and enjoying the built-in benefits offered by Cuna Mutual.

Loans were cancelled on death. Shares and savings were doubled at death, dependant on age, as well as other additional benefits including the stand-out APR of 12.68% on loans. The credit union concept didn't need selling. It needed to be awakened like a sleeping giant in Great Britain.

In my opinion, the Americans were looking for a front man and knew that I had already made presentations at conferences, free of charge, in the name of what I called being a good socialist. I loved the idea of putting our money into a pot with other like-minded people and sharing the profits amongst ourselves and not with the big banks.

The Association had to convince the Register of Friendly Societies that a common bond existed before registration. It was easier to make a case for a Police Federation, or fire fighters or council workers, but harder for the groups who really wanted and needed a credit union – communities.

I visited the home of the World Council of Credit Unions in Madison, Wisconsin as part of my induction and made two presentations. One was to the Board of Cuna Mutual and the other to a large audience of American credit union dignitaries. I received a standing ovation after explaining what I thought was needed to kick-start the British advance.

Sometime later, a female member of the ABCUL board wrote to America stating that I couldn't speak English properly. Perhaps that day at the presentation I had a Walter Winchell voiceover! Sure, I do not speak the Queen's English, but then again neither does Michael Caine, Ray

Winstone or the late great Bob Hoskins. And I do share with these guys, or at least their onscreen personas, a bit of fire in my 'Ned Kelly' and a passion for what I believe in.

I think I lasted three years at ABCUL, and for quite a few reasons I was not happy in my work. A typical week started on Monday early in the morning when I drove to a meeting in Luton, then Coventry in the afternoon, up to Birmingham ready for the next day's meetings. A couple of presentations, then over to Newcastle to visit a potential credit union and so on until Friday evening, if there wasn't a weekend seminar, make for home. Not exactly ideal for family life, what with waking up and being unsure where you were. But I didn't complain and played to my strengths. I was told that my weekend work was part of the job and no days in lieu could be taken. Always read the small print!

I was allocated an American liaison officer to assist my takeover and saw a great deal of him. He saw a great deal of one of my staff and married her.

In my time as CEO, I had two Presidents. The first was a reverend and the second an Australian lady. They were two completely different characters. The reverend was a nice man who admitted his knowledge of credit unions was limited. The lady had been inducted into the credit union lifestyle in Oz and was very knowledgeable, add to it haughty, interfering and constantly on the 'eau de' to the States about my shortcomings in her opinion.

I got on well with the ABCUL Board. They were happy with me and about to offer me a three year extended contract, when I was notified that a representative from America would be working with me. This, I knew, was the slippery slope, and whispers over the phone were coming to fruition. The representative was like a Siamese twin: in the office with me, out in the field with me. He was a charming man but I had the benefit of a street education. I knew what was coming.

There was a review of my job by various Irish credit union officials, headed by a top Yank. The outcome was along the lines of "We don't know what you do all day long." My forte was as a front man, so much so that when I was employed, I was told, hand on shoulder, "get out there and build it up". And when I was out there for most of the week, I had staff to run the office for me. I wanted to be judged on my development skills, not office skills, which in fairness, was what all and sundry knew I was employed to do. I was told my management style was good for the cab trade, but that it was ABCUL Board which should be running the Association, and that I was only there to implement their wishes.

Was I to sit and wait for once a month decisions from Board members who were only too pleased for me to run things on a day to day basis and continue their daily jobs?

The crunch came when I was asked to meet a top official in Madison. He complained that I wasn't listening to my advisors, to whom the Board was not listening to either. I explained that sometimes the USA way isn't maybe the British way.

I didn't 'buckle down' and remained, as usual, my own man. Unfortunately, the Americans were funding us and we couldn't bite the hand that feeds us. Plus, Britain really needed, and were grateful for, the American support. So I did the honourable thing and resigned. I still love the credit union and belong to my local Mosshill Credit Union. I hope the British credit union movement continues to grow and gives even more benefits to its membership.

CHAPTER ELEVEN
The South-East Golf Society

In the early eighties, my good friend and cab driver, Danny Sullivan, suggested we organise a once monthly golf outing for our fellow cab drivers. Danny arranged the venues and I was Treasurer. Little did we know the enjoyment it would bring us all. Every month around forty cab drivers would turn up at the course in the south of London, usually in Kent or Surrey. The competition was fierce and apart from the normal golf challenges, we added Best Dressed Man on the course and Best Dressed Man in the clubhouse.

Amongst its members, the society had a born comedian in Ralph Napolitano. Not obvious from his name, Ralph was a cheeky Londoner and a second generation Italian.

Big Charlie was in excess of twenty stone and had difficulty in looking the part in evening dress, so he opted to win Best Dressed Man on the course. Charlie was a gentle giant and had a Colonel Comb-Over hairstyle, a la Bobby Charlton. When the wind blew, his lacquered hair would stand up like a flat pancake.

We were playing at Purley Downs, a pleasant course in Surrey. Big Charlie came out of the dressing rooms in red trousers, red shirt and a red pullover. Little Ralph, probably five foot five, went up to Big Charlie, all of six foot two, and put an envelope in his mouth, saying, "What time is the first post collection?"

All the onlookers went into convulsions of laughter, Charlie made as if to clump Ralph and then smiled and said, "Later, later."

Another time, one of our golfers dressed completely in shades of green and was announced as the winner with the title 'Sir Robin of Sherwood'.

There was no stopping Little Ralphie. Once at Cherry Lodge Club, Micky W. displayed his arm that had had a tattoo removed. We all just nodded to show interest. Not Ralphie. He went up, took Micky's arm and said, "What was the tattoo?" And before Micky could answer, Ralphie asked, "Is there any truth to the rumour that they spelt 'Mum' wrong?"

One night at Dulwich and Sydenham Club, I entered the bar, sending myself up, to win the Best Dressed Man in the clubhouse. I sported a double-breasted blazer, dog-toothed check trousers, suede shoes and a button-down lilac shirt with a cravat and a glass monocle in one eye. The committee disqualified me on the grounds of using a prop – the monocle.

A couple of days later, Michael, the seventeen-year-old son of my good pal Johnny Blue Cab, phoned me. Michael was into fashion and he said, "Rog, I just bought a crevasse. Can you show me how to tie it?"

Big Charlie was the star of the society, a huge man who could hit a ball like a pro or shank it like the rest of us. We were playing at Ashdown Forest, and Charlie, Blue Cab and I were second out on the tee. Standing behind us, at a distance, were some of the boys, waiting to follow us out. Charlie got his Big Bertha out and found the trees on the left. He put another ball down and found the trees on the right. His third ball drove the green. Looking at me as if he had won the competition, he said, "Did you see that, Lewis?"

All the boys behind us were trying to calculate how many shots he had played. Trying to be diplomatic, I said,

"Charlie, one swallow doesn't make a summer. Let's not hold the rest up any more."

The only time I won the competition was at Wimbledon Park, opposite the tennis grounds. Incidentally, on that day Charlie didn't drive the green; he drove Centre court. Luckily, it was February.

I was playing with Terry Cottle, who was from a good southeast London family. At the seventh hole, there was a lake and it was a par three. I took a seven-iron and the ball skimmed the water, bouncing onto the green a foot away from the flag. I putted for a two. In the clubhouse, it was announced that the winner was Barnes Wallace (him of the bouncing bomb fame).

Every year the Society had a knock-out competition, which had to be played between our monthly meetings at a mutually convenient course agreed by the two opponents. In the event, it was Irish Frank versus Terry H, and to be held at the club in Chislehurst, at the exquisitely beautiful Camden Place. Napoleon III and his family resided here while in exile and received all the top luminaries of the day, including Queen Victoria.

There was animosity between Frank and Terry, so Danny Sullivan agreed to referee the game. On the first tee, trouble brewed and a fight started, resulting in both golfers falling from the raised tee and one pressing his club against the other's throat. Danny, all of eight stone, tried to separate them. Two members arrived to tee off. Danny looked up and said nonchalantly, "Play through, please."

The only snobbery I encountered was when booking some venues. Once I rang to book and the secretary was happy to be told 'forty for golf' and the evening meal. When I asked about the size of the car park, explaining that we were all London taxi drivers, he declined to take the booking. Silly man.

We always spent big at the bar, and, with four in the back and a driver, everyone took a turn to drive and not drink.

The Society ran for years until the recession in the nineties when taxi drivers were forced to work long hours to make up loss of income.

CHAPTER TWELVE
The Mafia

After visiting the New York drivers to investigate the workings of their credit union, I travelled to Boston to look at how the Scholarship Fund operated for the cab drivers' children. The Treasurer of the Boston Cab Association was a slim, bespeckled man, aged about forty-five called Felix Testa. We got on well together and he took me to lunch in Quincy Market. During the meal I told him I was looking for a book about Jimmy Hoffa, the Teamsters boss.

He said 'Who's Jimmy Hoffa?' which at the time was a name that was on every American's lips since his disappearance in July 1975 off the face of the earth.

We finished lunch and I went about other business, thinking what a good guy Felix was.

We exchanged business cards and one week later I received a book titled 'The Hoffa Wars'.

With the book was a letter from Felix. I wrote back and thanked him.

A year later I was on holiday in the States, touring with my family, and drove to Boston to visit Felix and to repay lunch. When I went into the reception of the Cab Association, the Receptionist remembered me and took me outside. I asked if Felix was in and she said in whispered tones "Felix isn't here anymore. His family were involved in a Mafia war." I didn't know if 'here anymore' meant living or changed jobs. Judging by the fear in her voice I didn't labour the point.

Two Christmas's ago my wife bought me a book called 'Blood and Honour' by George Anastasia. To my surprise, it was about the Testa family. I read it twice and I am happy to say that despite several of the family being despatched, there was no mention of Felix. Thank God.

Any book that is about the Mafia's rackets in America always seems to include penetration in the unions and trade associations, and Boston seemed to highlight it for me.

After the LTDA Credit Union was formed, I was the invited guest of the League of Mutual Taxi Owners (LOMTO) Credit Union and asked to speak at their AGM in the Catskills. It was a grand affair and the New York drivers and their families took over the hotel for the long weekend. The food was outstanding and the leisure facilities second to none: swimming, gym, tennis, racket ball and golf.

A good friend of mine wanted to join me and visit New York, and as he paid his way there was no objection to him coming.

On the second day in the Catskills we were out first in a four ball with the LOMTO secretary, Howie Fogal, and their Treasurer. On the first day Howie hit his ball into the bushes and said 'Mulligan.' At that time, in 1982, I looked about thinking he was calling to someone called Mulligan. Then he explained that during a round everyone can claim one mis-hit shot off the tee and take it as a freebie. I indulged this quaint ruling and used it when I lost my ball off the tee into a small lake.

Behind us was another four-ball, who were introduced to us at a pit stop for drinks after the nineth hole. I shook hands and had a nice conversation with Carmine, Salvatore, Paulie and Frankie. They told me they were in the taxi insurance business which made sense of their being with a cab driver group in the Catskills.

That evening, at a six-course dinner, I noticed the taxi insurance men at the next table with four much younger ladies who had dresses that elevated their 'thruppenny bits' almost at a straight line. My travelling companion was intrigued and thought that the ladies were the daughters of the four just men. I think the Italian for the ladies is 'goomas' or mistresses. My friend got a smile reciprocated from one of the ladies. Howie was alarmed and said to me out of the corner of his mouth 'Tell him to behave himself. That's the Mob.'

Later that evening I was standing by a piano at the edge of the dance floor drinking and listening to the band when one of the ladies in question approached me and said in a Brooklyn accent 'Hey, man, you wanna dance?'

'Thanks, darlin' but I've got a wooden leg,' I said limping away.

CHAPTER THIRTEEN
The Movies and Me

Self-praise is no praise, but even though I say it myself, I have stored lots of useless information about the silver screen, mainly specialising in films featured at the first Oscars ceremony in May 1929 , those made from 1927 – 1928, until the late eighties.

I was at home one New Year's Eve and the phone went. It was a call from my pal, Micky Murray, in Canada.

"I'm having an argument with my father in law. Can you settle it?"

"Who was the bird with The Duke in 'North to Alaska'?"

"Capucine."

"Thanks mate. Happy New Year." Click. End of conversation.

I love meeting other film buffs to see what they know and to test my knowledge against theirs. There are several hardy annuals that most buffs should be able to answer. Here are ten of them:

1. Name the 'Magnificent Seven'.

2. Name the 'Twelve Angry Men'.

3. What was Oliver Hardy's middle name?

4. Who was the film star sister of Joan Fontaine?

5. What was the real name of Doris Day?

6. Which double act were born Crochett and Levich?

7. Who are the only two male actors to win back to back Academy Awards in two consecutive years, and name the films?

8. What was the name of Jack Palance's character in 'Shane'?

9. For what film in 1942 did Jimmy Cagney win an Oscar?

10. Who was the baby being christened in the cathedral at the end of 'The Godfather, Part 1?

One night I picked up Robin Ray, son of Ted the old comedian. Robin ran a television show called 'Film Buff of the Year', which I wanted to be on. He soon brought me down to earth and found my weakest links. I asked him how good did you need to be to go on the show. From the back of the cab he fired questions at me, amongst which were sci-fi and horror films, which I wouldn't cross the road to watch. He got out of the cab in Knightsbridge and said, "You're good but no cigar."

I only ever watch films that are believable and read books that are factual, showing up my limitations in the field of competitiveness.

The golden days of Hollywood produced class acts and as a kid I went to the 'dolly mixtures' as often as I could. There were places called The Eros, the Prince of Wales, the Splendid and the Ritz, and they all smelled wonderful with carpet in the foyer and down the aisle. At the other end of the scale, there were the 'bug hutches' with poor entrances and rotten seats, but no matter what the surroundings, you still went to see Errol Flynn in Lincoln green or Duke in his cavalry uniform with Victor McLaglen as Sergeant Quincannon.

It was in one of these bug hutches in Deptford High Street that I witnessed in full flow a character called Chopper Green. Chopper was a king amongst the Teddy Boys: big Tony Curtis hair cut and a warrior, who happened to live opposite the side door of the picture palace. Our gang, ranging in age from ten to twelve, were all sitting in the tanner seats, mouths open watching a pirate – Douglas Fairbanks – put his sword in the top of a sail of a pirate ship and travel down to the deck. Suddenly the exit door flew open from the outside, the dark room flooding with light. There stood Chopper Green in full regalia: draped jacket and drain pipe 'council houses'. He came in, ripped a seat off and took it home for firewood for his mum. The attendants stayed schtum.

A common occurrence was Chopper slipping in from the exit door without paying a tanner entrance fee. He only left when his mum came in the exit and shouted "Chopper, you're dinner's ready".

Deptford was a rough place and I went to school there for five years, learning much about streetwise. We couldn't wait for the weekend so we could go to the Saturday morning pictures for kids only. We were the minors of the ABC and every Saturday morning we marvelled at Pearl White, tied up on a railway track with a steam train hurtling towards her, or Flash Gordon pursued by the evil Emperor Ming. Flash was always in a precarious position but in the next week's episode he always escaped. We had Stan and Ollie and the Three Stooges but not the Marx Brothers who probably were too sophisticated for our young brains.

But above all we had Roy Rogers, Dale Evans, Trigger and Gabby Hayes. What adventure! Thousands of miles away in the Wild West our hero on the best horse ever seen always beat the baddies. His real name was Len Sly and he became a legend, only second – for me – to The Duke, John Wayne.

The Saturday picture show was magical. I remember that no one wanted to sit in the last row of the cheap seats because it had an aisle behind it, and a little bastard we called Froggy would crawl in the dark and hit people on the head with his fist. The kids all sang our song as the words came up on the screen. In summer, some of the poorer kids came along in their school trousers with braces, boots and wooly socks but no shirt, which I think was being washed, ready for school on Monday. The saddest thing I recall was a little girl came out of the cinema, got run over by a car and lost a leg. It all stopped when I became over age, and so left all the wonderment to the next generation.

The love of cinema also got me and Monkey Ford expelled from the Cub Scouts. My Mum had bought me my green Cubs uniform, complete with a woggle and scarf. I loved the games in the Cubs' hut, learning to tie knots, going on parade, helping old people across the road. But it all came to an abrupt end.

It was 'bob a job' week, where the Cubs knocked on street doors and asked if there was any work that needed to be done, such as cleaning windows, cutting the grass or going to the shops. The customer signed your card and wrote down what was paid for the task. I was teamed up with Monkey, and we took about a pound between us. He suggested "Let's go to the 'dolly mixtures' and some 'oily rags'. I was all of eight years old; Monkey was nearly ten. We bought a packet of five fags, and I was as sick as a dog.

Come Friday, we reported to the Cub hut and the 'Akela' – a Hattie Jacques lookalike – asked Monkey where our money was. "We lost it, Miss." Both of us were drummed out, never to become a fully-fledged Scout. The nearest thing to Baden Powell I ever became, was his name was Cockney rhyming slang for towel.

Over the years as I grew older, my favourite film stars changed, and I began to recognise the difference between an actor and a film star, in the same way as the difference between a boxer and a fighter. I recognised the vast talent of British film actors: Olivier, Gielgud, Richardson, Alastair Sim, Attenborough, Mills and Guinness. But they didn't connect with me as a Londoner who didn't speak the Queen's English.

Cockney parts were given to a Hooray Henrys who tried to do a working class accent but who finished by sounding like Dick Van Dyke in 'Mary Poppins'. The only people I could relate to were Harry Fowler, Alfie Bass and an old actor, Wally Patch. Even Sid James in 'The Lavender Hill Mob' was a South African playing a Cockney.

Then it happened. Not straightaway – it took Maurice Micklewhite playing Gonville Bromhead in 'Zulu' as an upper class Johnnie before he could be himself. Then came Bob Hoskins and my favourite, Ray Winstone, who despite being a Hammer is a class act. Now, at long last, the Cockneys had someone to relate to.

I could never understand why Dick Van Dyke got the part in 'Mary Poppins' when Tommy Steele, who could sing and dance, would not have had to put on a 'mockney' accent.

Caine in 'Alfie', 'Get Carter', Hoskins in 'The Long Good Friday', and Winstone in 'Scum' and 'Nil by Mouth' were outstanding. Thank God for the above three, and the newcomers making their mark, speaking in their native tongue.

Over the years, I also loved the American cinema and its great directors: Billy Wilder, William Wyler, John Ford, John Huston, Sam Pekinpah, Francis Ford Coppella, Michael Curtiz, and – my favourite – Martin Scorcese.

My all time favourite film is 'On the Waterfront'. How could it not be a great film? Based on the novel by Budd Schulberg and directed by Elia Kazan, the cast includes Carl Malden, Leif Erikson, Martin Balsam and Rod Steiger. There isn't a bad actor in it. Eva Marie Saint made her debut in it and won an Oscar, as did Marlon Brando. But the man for me is Lee J. Cobb, playing the corrupt longshoreman union boss, John Friendly, aka John Skelly.

The book of the film was based on fact. 'Tough Tony' Anastasia ran the New York docks on kickbacks and bribes under the protection of his brother, Albert Anastasia, who was head of Murder Inc. and met his end in a barber's chair by a mob hit.

I make no excuse for listing my twenty favourite films in the hope that one of my grandkids will follow me and love of cinema as part of their education and as a worthwhile hobby. So here, in no particular order, after number one:

1.	**On the Waterfront**	**1954**
	Marlon Brando	
2.	**Twelve Angry Men**	**1957**
	Henry Fonda	
3.	**Raging Bull**	**1980**
	Robert De Niro	
4.	**The Godfather I**	**1972**
	All star cast	
5.	**The Godfather II**	**1974**
	All star cast	
6.	**The Quiet Man**	**1952**
	The 'Duke', Maureen O Hara	
7.	**Yankee Doodle Dandy**	**1942**
	James Cagney	
8.	**Casablanca**	**1942**
	Humphrey Bogart	

9. **The Searchers** 1956
   The 'Duke'

10. **The Scent of a Woman** 1993
    Al Pacino

11. **Goodfellas** 1993
    Robert De Niro, Joe Pesci

12. **True Romance** 1993
    Christian Slater

13. **Angels with Dirty Faces** 1938
    James Cagney

14. **Sleepers** 1996
    Brad Pitt, Robert De Niro

15. **A Bronx Tale** 1993
    Robert De Niro

16. **Riffifi** 1955
    Jean Servais

17. **Sweet Smell of Success** 1957
    Tony Curtis, Burt Lancaster

18. **Frankie & Johnnie** 1991
    Al Pacino

19. The Apartment   **1960**

Jack Lemon, Shirley McLaine

20. Zulu   **1964**

Michael Caine

By the time my Grandkids are old enough to appreciate my love of the above films, some will be sixty to seventy years old. By putting them in writing, I hope they won't be forgotten.

Film Question Answers

1. Yul Brynner, Steve McQueen, Horst Buchholz, Brad Dexter, Charles Bronson, Robert Vaughn, James Coburn

2. Henry Fonda, Jack Warden, Lee J Cobb, Ed Begley, E.G. Marshall, Edward Binns, Joseph Sweeney, Martin Balsam, Jack Klugman, John Fiedler, George Voskovec and Robert Webber

3. Norvell

4. Olivia de Havilland

5. Doris Mary Ann Kappelhoff

6. Martin and Lewis

7. Spencer Tracy: 'Captain's Courageous', 1937 and 'Boys Town', 1938; Tom Hanks: 'Philadelphia', 1993 and 'Forrest Gump', 1994

8. Jack Wilson

9. Yankee Doodle Dandy

10. Sophia Ford Coppola

CHAPTER FOURTEEN
The Three Ladies

'They are not long, the days of wine and roses'
Ernest Dowson

There were three special ladies in my life. Two are gone, and each of them suffered the biggest and worst illness on the planet.

Marian was my first lady and fiancée for four years and as we grew up together, it was inevitable we would grow apart because of our strong, individual personalities. She was a class act. Her dress sense and style top drawer. It was always a pleasure to be seen with her. Marian was an achiever. At a very early age she had her own hair dressing salon, her own car, and was always immaculately dressed. But we always found arguments were second nature between us. I was never one to sit quietly in the corner and accept various points of view. Subsequently, our relationship had more ups and downs than Tower Bridge. The engagement was off more times than a stripper's bra. Eventually, Marian and I did the right thing for the both of us, and she gave me back my ring. Marian married and had two children. She died in London Bridge Hospital at the age of fifty.

My first wife, Janet, and mother to my two children beat skin cancer back in 1976 after dreadful skin grafts and mind boggling battles with fear of any life expectancy. We remain friends today, forty years on, but if Janet feels that I have not treated my kids in the way a father should, she is not slow to tell me. I hasten to add these instances are few and far between because of the love I have for my kids. I was always a good father; perhaps not always a good husband. I tended to buy my right to follow my job.

No marriages are perfect. There are always cracks that can heal or grow longer, and wider. It takes two to keep a relationship together. In our case, I was never there. I spent ten years building a cab trade organisation, the LTDA, and missed a lot of my children's fun and development. The cause of our divorce after twenty-three years really had little to do with Janet. I was 99% to blame. She was and is a good mother and grandmother who has the benefit of being able to see her family regularly. It was a big price for me to pay four hundred miles away, but nevertheless my choice.

The reason I got divorced from Janet was simple and at the same time, very complicated. I fell in love with Pat who lived four hundred miles away in Scotland. Whoever invented the telephone, Alexander Graham Bell or Antonio Meucci, I owe a big **Thank You!.**

Pat and I first met in 1979 at a Credit Union AGM in Blackpool. I represented the LTDA and Pat was a delegate for Mosshill. I was impressed with her knowledge and ability as a volunteer for her local thriving credit union, as well as with her looks and style. That was as far as it went until ten years later when we met again. This time she was the full time manager of Mosshill Credit Union and I was the CEO for ABCUL.

There is no point in labouring what followed: we moved in together and left our previous spouses. It was pure and simple. We both loved each other and it remained that way until her untimely passing in 2013.

At the time of writing, I have been a widower for thirty months. Her passing is still a very bitter pill to swallow for me, my stepdaughters whom I love, her friends and family, leaving us all to believe there is no fairness to life. I could fill the next ten pages with Pat's attributes but suffice it to say she was feisty, which I loved, the most kind hearted person I have ever met and she made me the most wonderful wife. She was also a wonderful mother and grandmother to Shonna, Cherelle and Marley, respectively. I'm not an especially religious man but there's a passage in Proverbs that could have been written especially for Pat, that a good woman "is more precious than rubies. The heart of her husband doth safely trust in her. She will do him good all the days of her life".

Living in Scotland

When Pat and I made the decision to live together, it wasn't the easiest choice for us to make. I loved London, and still miss my kids, grandkids, friends and my season ticket at Millwall F.C., in that order.

I had resigned my position at ABCUL and was working at my first love – driving around the streets of London in a black cab. Was it better for Pat to come down to the Big Smoke and give up the job she loved at the Credit Union, or for me to move to Scotland? We decided I would cross the border and start a new life at the age of fifty. I have never regretted the decision. Scotland is a lovely country and it is a good place to live and inevitably for me to die.

Both my parents and Pat's ashes are in a local crematorium, where provision is made for me to join them.

Before I moved to Scotland, my original plan was for Daniel to take my ashes to the middle of Tower Bridge where the bascules meet. My ashes were to be scattered into the Thames at receding tide, carried downstream past Deptford and Millwall. The significance of the bridge is that Mum came from one side and my Dad the other. But now I'll join my parents and Pat in the Holytown crematorium.

Underneath, it still remains you can take the boy out of London, but you can't take London out of the boy. With apologies to Rupert Brooke for the slight alteration, "When I should die, think only this of me, that there's some corner of Scotland that is forever London". So, after twenty-odd years, I still proudly retain my accent and haven't adopted the local phrases or differences in words, for example, weans for children, snib for doorlock, miserable for mean, asking 'How?' when you mean 'Why?'

I've come across a bit of anti-English behaviour, but I still believe that working class men have the same outlook in life, whether they are Cockneys, Scousers, Geordies or Scots. They love their football, betting, a drink, their country, telling jokes and have a good sense of humour.

So, when Pat and I became a couple, I went to London for ten days a month to get a living on the cab and sleeping on the floor at my parents' one bedroom flat in southeast London. I worked for ten days, came home and did nothing for twenty days until one day I went to get my annual tax returns done as a sole trader at Martin Cordell Limited, a leading firm of accountants in Bow, London.

I had known Martin Cordell previously from when I was at the LTDA, and he knew I had a financial background as treasurer of the LTDA, the LTDA Credit Union and as CEO of ABCUL. He asked if I was willing to work in Scotland for him, undertaking the accounts of licensed cab drivers.

After training, it helped that I had knowledge of the workings of the cab trade.

Martin opened two offices: one in Glasgow and one in Edinburgh, and I started with no clients. Today, Martin Cordell Ltd has nine hundred drivers on its books in Scotland, and its business is still growing. I work with a very capable young man, Paul Mitchell, who has become a good work mate and friend. I enjoy meeting five different cab drivers a day, and there is always good banter. When Pat passed on, everyone thought I would return to London. Despite offers to move back from my daughter, Alex in Earls Colne, Essex, and my son Daniel in South-east London, I decided to see out my days in Mossend, Lanarkshire.

Pat provided us with a beautiful flat, and as long as I am able to work and function on my own, I will remain in my adopted country. I am lucky to have good friends who call me regularly, thanks to John Francis (JBC); Brian Owen, Martin and Irene Harvey and Flo Wiltshire all in London, from further afield, the Wardens who live in France and Micky M in Canada.

Up until now, life has been good to me. The future is unwritten.

'What we hope ever to do with ease, we learn to do first with diligence.'

Dr Samuel Johnson

TALES FROM THE RANKS AND BEYOND | 371

My beloved wife Pat

APPENDIX
Rhyming Slang Translated

A.

Alan Whicker's – Knickers

Anna May Wong – Strong (as in overstepping the mark)

Apples and Pears or Apples – Stairs

Aunt Nelly – Smelly

Army and Navy – Gravy

Arthur Conan Doyle – Boil

Acker Bilk – Milk

Almond Rocks – Socks

B.

Bottle and Glass – Arse

Battle Cruiser – Boozer, as in Pub or Bar

Belle Vue – Spew or Vomit

Billy Bunter – Punter

Boat Race – Face

Bon Marche – Moustache

Brahms and Lizst – Pissed, or inebriated

Brian Curvis – Service

Bull and Cow – Row

Bubble and Squeak – Greek

Barnet or Barnet Fair – Hair

Biscuits and Cheese – Knees

Bob Hope – Soap

Ben Gazi – Khazi which means Latrine in Swahili

Brandy Snaps – Jap as in Japanese person or people

Blaydon Races – Braces

C.

Cassius Clay – A spray, as in spray paint job on a car

Charlie Chan – Tan

China Plate – Mate

Council Houses – Trousers

Christopher Lee – Pee

Callard and Bowsers – Trousers

Cows Calf's – Half (ten shillings)

D.

Daily Mail – Tail, as in someone is on my tail

Dolly Mixures – The pictures as in the cinema

Donald Duck – Luck

Doris Day – Gay

Duke of Kent – Rent

Duchess or Duchess of Fife – Wife

Dig in the Grave – Shave

E.

Eau de or Eau de Cologne – Telephone

Elephants Trunk or Elephants – Drunk

F.

Filbert – Nut, as in "to lose your filbert" (to lose your temper or composure)

Forsythe Saga – Lager

Farmer Giles – Piles

G.

George Segal – A legal, which in the Cab trade means that the customer has paid the precise fare only without giving the driver a tip

Greengages – Wages

Gunga Din – Thin

Gregory Peck – Neck

H.

Hackney Wick – Sick

Hattie Jacques or Hatties – Brakes, as in a car

Hickory or Hickory Dickory Dock – Clock

Harris Tweed – Swede

Holy Ghost – Toast

Harry Lime – Time as in, what time of the day is it?

I.

Ice Cream Freezer – Geezer

Irish Jig – Wig

I Suppose – Nose

J.

Jack Doyle – Oil

Jam Jar – Car

Jekyll and Hyde – Snide

Joe Baxi – Taxi

K.
Khyber Pass or Khyber – Arse

Kipper and Bloater or Kipper – Photo

L.
Lady Godiva – Fiver, or five pound note

Lillian Skinner or Lillian – Dinner

Linen Draper – Paper, as in newspaper

**Lionel Blair`s** – Flare`s, the style of trousers

Lord of the Manor – A tanner, meaning a sixpence piece

Leamington Spa – Bra

Lillian Gish – Fish

M.
Moriarty or Mori – Party

N.

Newington Butts – Guts

Nanny Goat – Coat

Ned Kelly – Belly

Nelson Eddies or Nelsons – Readies, meaning ready cash

Nelson Riddle – Piddle

Niagara`s or Niagara Falls – meaning Balls (male anatomy)

Northants – Pants

Norton and Gold – Cold

O.

Oily Rags – Fags as in cigarettes

One Hundred to Thirty – Dirty

Orchestral Stalls – Balls

Oxford Scholar or an Oxford – Dollar, meaning five shillings

P.
Peckham Rye – Tie

Pie and Mash – Flash, in the sense of showy display of clothes or behaviour

Pint and Half – Scarf

Plaster or Plaster of Paris – Aris as in Aristotle as in bottle, as in bottle and glass as in arse

Pony – £25.00

Penny Stamp – Tramp

Petrol Tank – Yank as in American person

Q.
Queens Park Ranger – Stranger

R.
Richard the Third – Bird, as in your girlfriend or young women in general

Rubber Dubs – Pub

Ruby Murray or Ruby – Curry

Radio Rental – Mental

S.

Sandy McNab – Taxi Cab

Sherbet Dab – Taxi Cab

Sir John Barbirollis – Trolleys, as in the heavy carts pulled by men in the markets

Skin and Blisters – Sisters

Stand at Ease – Cheese

Stoke on Trent – Bent, as in crooked or untrustworthy

Sky Rocket or Sky – Pocket

St Louis or St Louis blues – Shoes

Sexton Blake – Steak

Syrup of Fig – Wig

T.

Todd Slone – On your own

Todd Slaughter – Daughter

Tate and Lyle – Style

Tit for Tat – Hat

Tommy Trinder – Window

Tomfoolery or Tom – Jewellery

Tonne – £100.00

Thruppenny Bits – Tits

V.
Vincent Price – Ice

Vera Lynn – Gin

W.
Whistle and Flute – Suit

Z.
Zigs or Zigfield Follies – Dollies

REST IN PEACE

While this book was being written three special people to me passed on.

My beloved wife Pat, my pal since my teens and fellow cabbie Peter Warden and big Barry Addinall, a London cab driver I met while doing the Knowledge, who I remained friends with for forty years.

Roger Lewis